Jennifer Guidi

Full Moon

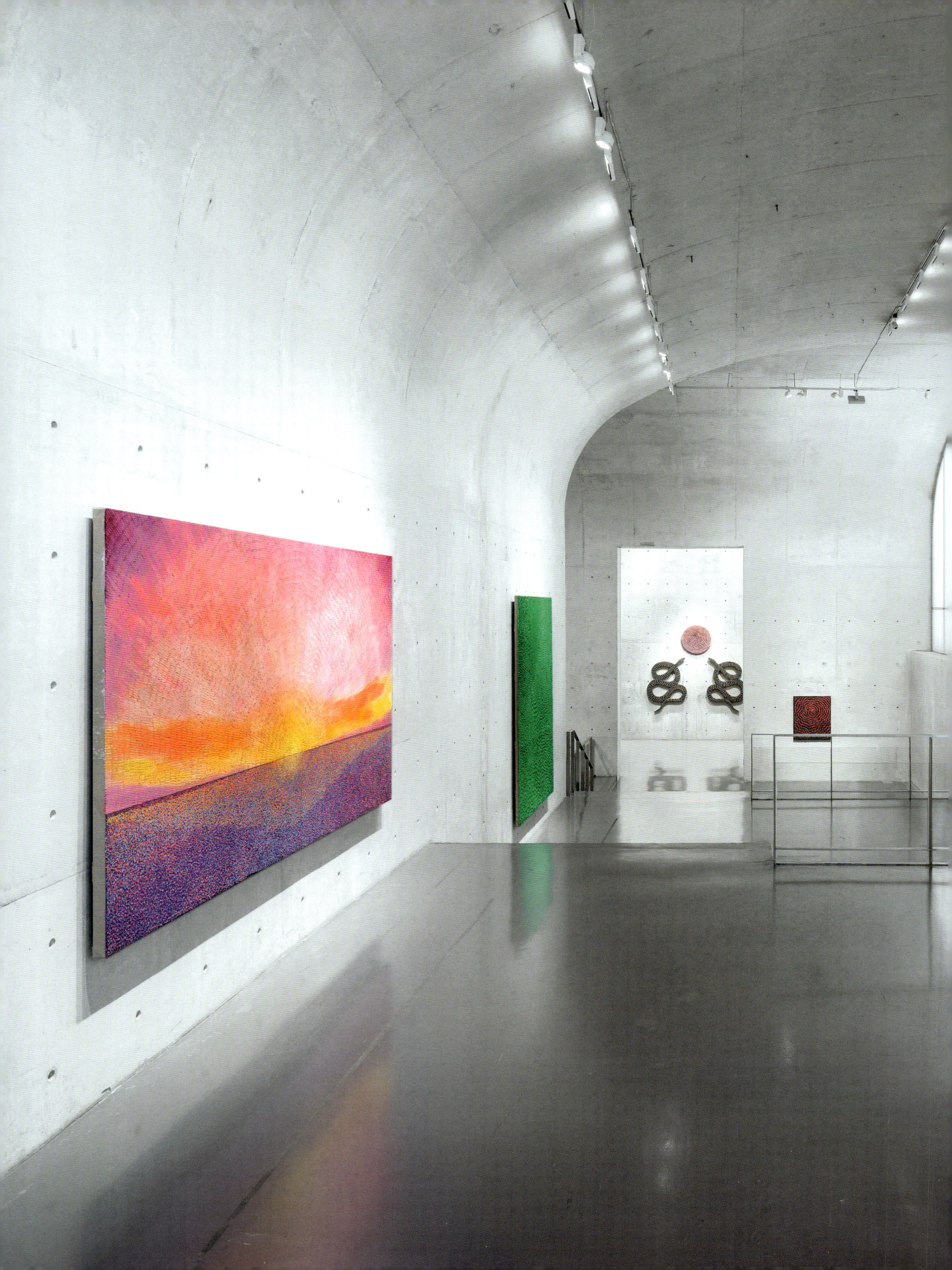

Jennifer Guidi

Full Moon

SKIRA

Cover
Moonlight and Love (Painted Pink Sand, Black-Dark Blue-Purple-Pink-Green-Yellow Sky, Yellow-Purple-Dark Purple-Pink-Red Mountain), detail, 2021
Sand, acrylic and oil on linen
21 x 15 inches

Chief Editor
Flavio Del Monte, MASSIMODECARLO

Art Director
Luigi Fiore

Editorial Coordination
Eva Vanzella

Copy Editor
Andrew Ellis

Layout
Sara Marcon

Photo Credits
All artwork photography by Brica Wilcox
except pp. 42–43: Flying Studio
and pp. 44–45: Brian Forrest
Installation images by Shaunley Hon
Courtesy of the artist

First published in Italy in 2024 by Skira editore S.p.A.
Palazzo Casati Stampa
via Torino 61
20123 Milano
Italy
www.skira.net

Printed and bound in Italy.
First edition

ISBN: 978-88-572-5107-3

Distributed in USA, Canada, Central & South America by ARTBOOK | D.A.P., 75 Broad Street, Suite 630, New York, NY 10004, USA.
Distributed elsewhere in the world by Thames and Hudson Ltd., 181A High Holborn, London WC1V 7QX, United Kingdom

This catalogue was produced by MASSIMODECARLO and published on the occasion of the exhibition
Jennifer Guidi – Full Moon
July 1 – October 16, 2022
Long Museum (West Bund)
No. 3398, Longteng Avenue, Xuhui District, Shanghai, China
www.thelongmuseum.org

Exhibition Curator
Wang Wei

Long Museum Director
Wang Wei

Research Department
Ye Wenxiu, Lu Jin, Gu Xianting

Exhibition Department
Zhang Jingjie, Xie Zhihao, Xin Yishan, Li Fangzhou, Zhao Zinan, Wang Yu

Collect and Display Department
He Jiaxi, Wen Bin, Liu Zikang, Hong Xiaole

Business Development Department
Zhang Wenmao, Lu Huihong, Zhang Qian

Design Department
Zhou Xiangying

Image Department
Han Xiaoyi, Yang Yi

Administration Department
Zhang Xiaoxiao, Liu Shujie, Guo Ziyi, Chen Dong, Jin Meiting, Zhu Lan, Lin Kun, Qiu Yanfeng, Peng Danni, Huang Luyao, Wu Mushuang, Chen Baojun

Finance Department
Huang Lu, Chen Hui, Huang Cunli, Su Hua, Nan Ling

Engineering Department
Jiang Weibing, Tian Mingjin, Jin Xi

Contents

Jennifer Guidi: Full Moon

This catalogue documents the exhibition *Full Moon*, the first institutional solo exhibition in China by Los Angeles-based artist Jennifer Guidi, which took place at The Long Museum in Shanghai from July 1st until October 16, 2022. The exhibition is a survey of the artist's work to date and premiered a number of important new paintings: *Full Moon* epitomizes Guidi's practice and the evolution of her artistic process to date.

Guidi's immersive work operates within both the physical and metaphysical world. Her abstract compositions refer to the natural world literally and visually as she mixes sand with paint to depict arresting natural and cosmological phenomena. Her surroundings of Los Angeles, where she set up her studio after graduating from the School of the Art Institute of Chicago, are palpable through her work: the immense skies of California filled with the fleeting hues of sunrises and sunsets, the particular hazy light of Los Angeles that blurs colors together, and casts deep shadows and the mountains she passes daily on the way to her studio. Her practice is however deeply rooted in what also lies beyond physical surroundings, in the spiritual and metaphysical worlds. Each of her paintings is an "energy source" indebted to the power of vibrations, and her works incorporate recurring symbols related to Western and Eastern religions, ancient civilizations and the esoteric sciences. Guidi's very process of creating these serene, repetitive works is akin to a meditative practice. Reveling in external and internal symmetry in her work, such as sunrise and sunset, light and dark, these ideas sit alongside a scientific study of geometry and color theory, creating works that are not only visually in harmony but are epistemologically balanced too.

Always attracted to sand as a material, Guidi experimented with translating sand to canvas as a permanent medium, taking a few years to find the recognizable pattern that is now synonymous with her work. The highly textured works are created either by pressing divots with a dowel into a thick layer of wet sand, the "sand mandalas," or by starting with a smooth sand layer and painting the mandala on top, the "universe mandalas." A formative moment for her composition when "everything changed," came after watching Tibetan monks make sand mandalas, where patterns radiate from one central point. Guidi moved from using horizontal lines as the foundation of her composition along which she placed stitch-like marks, to making concentric repeated and formulated holes that radiate from a central focal point. They appeal to our somatic senses, the regular indentations capture the artist's corporeal presence in the work and encourage awareness of our own bodies' movement. The meditative sense of calm Guidi reaches during the creative act suffuses through her work, drawing us into her harmonious and immersive compositions. The tangibility of Guidi's movements and state of mind within the works makes them in part a self-portrait, with her presence forever fixed amongst the grains of sand.

The artist's fascination with light is inextricably tied to her attentiveness to color. The visible light spectrum is formed of all the colors of the rainbow, each wavelength of light vibrates at a different frequency to produce a different color. This idea forms the basis of her chromatic explorations and drew her to a study of chakra methodologies, an idea from early Hinduism. Chakras are energy centers within the human body, each giving off a different vibration, like the colors in the visible light spectrum. "Chakra" in Sanskrit translates to "wheel" or "circle," linking the spiritual idea to that of the nineteenth-century invention of color wheels and broader color theory, which associated specific color pairings with emotions, and explored in detail connections between nature and color. Read through these multiple lenses Guidi's investigation of a rainbow spectrum of color is therefore more than an exploration of pure pigment, but rather a reflection on emotion, shape, nature and philosophy.

The circle predominates Guidi's creative input, geometrically present in the repeated holes, and symbolically representative of the sun and moon. Other shapes recur throughout her work, as an exploration of pure geometry and for their diverse symbolism. Triangles represent California's mountains and refer to the allusions surrounding Ancient Egyptian pyramids. Guidi is drawn to the symbol of the serpent, relevant to ancient mythologies and mysticism. Their particularly complex symbolism represents rebirth, creativity and immortality through shedding of the skin and as the rod of Asclepius, the Ancient Greek god of healing, and consequent use as a symbol of medicine. Guidi uses shaped canvases to explore these forms and meanings, grouping symbols together in tandem and opposition to create a dialogue between their formal lines and to forge new meanings. These works are an innovative take on the traditional composition of diptychs and triptychs in paintings, using entirely separate canvases to create these formations, constructing works that lie somewhere between painting, sculpture, and design.

The title of the exhibition, *Full Moon*, emphasizes the cosmological and mystical roots of Jennifer Guidi's practice; the moon is like life: constantly changing; it is representative of peace, prosperity, harmony and good fortune; the full moon is a time to be receptive and to connect, which we are motivated to do throughout the exhibition. We are encouraged through engaging with her mandala-like works, not only to travel outward to be transported into distant landscapes and watch sunsets through her eyes, but also to travel inward to connect with our minds and spirits. During the full moon we are guided by unusually powerful light, symbolizing, much like the balance strived for in her work, a moment of unity between two dualities, where light can be found in darkness.

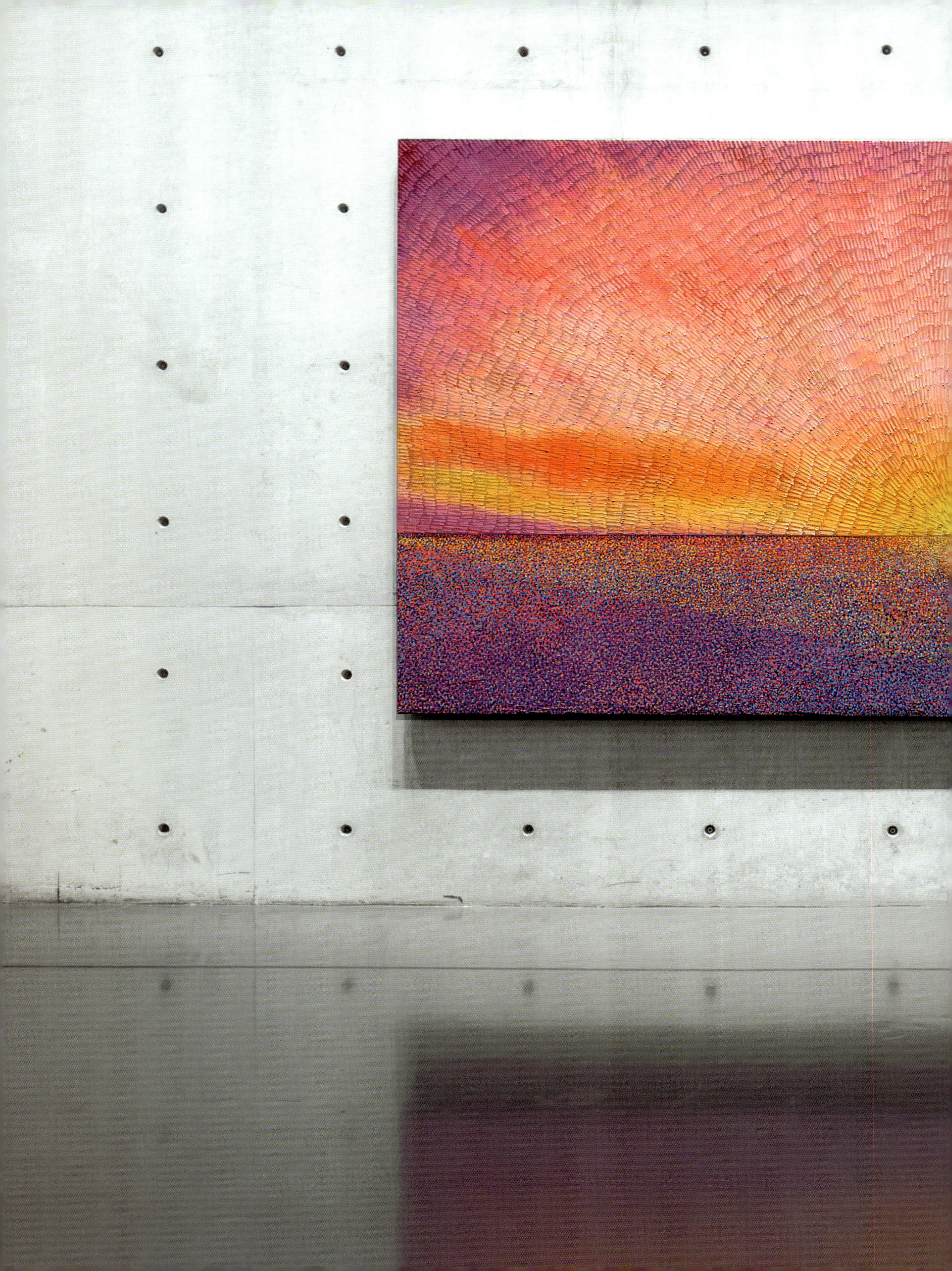

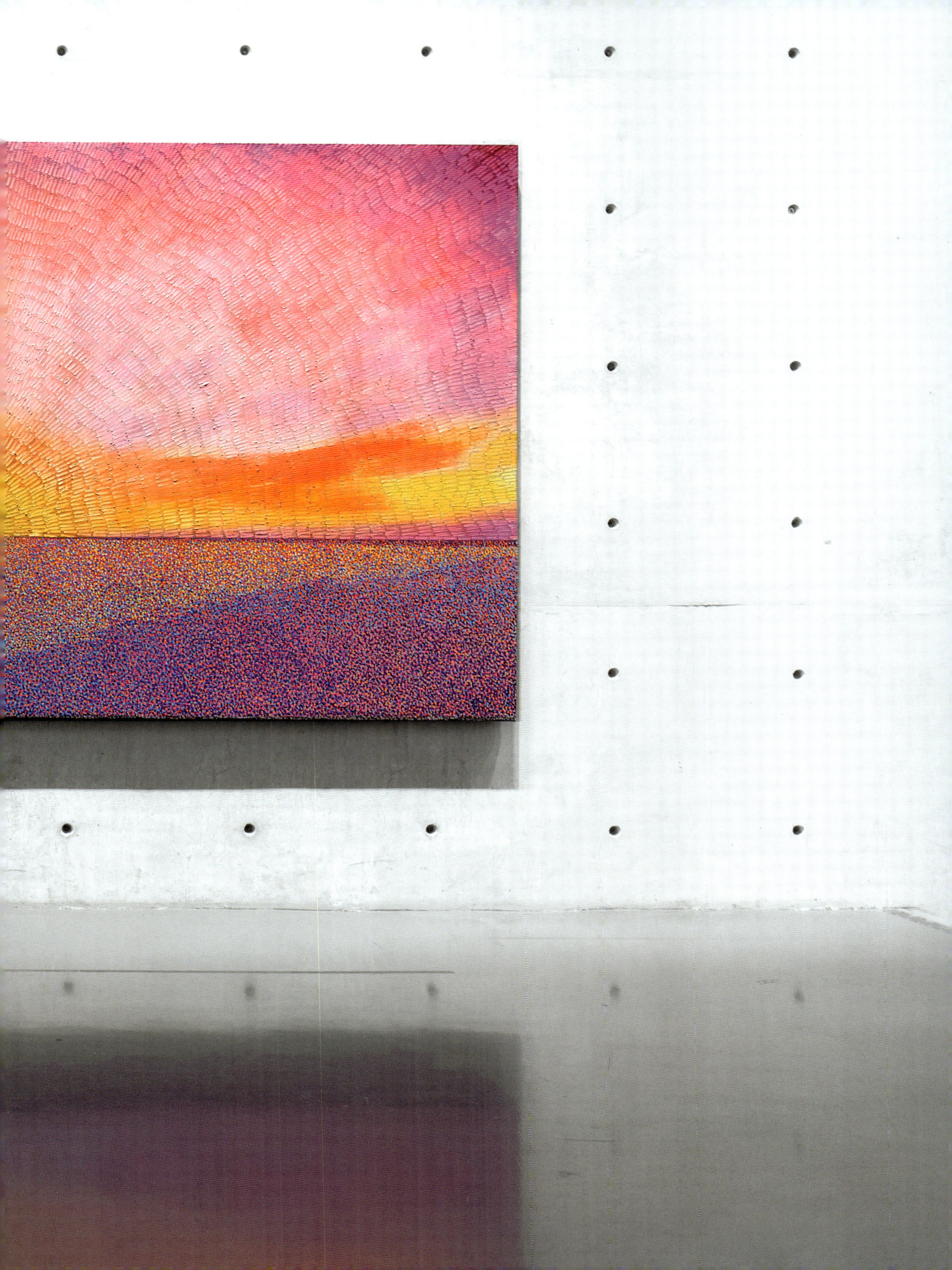

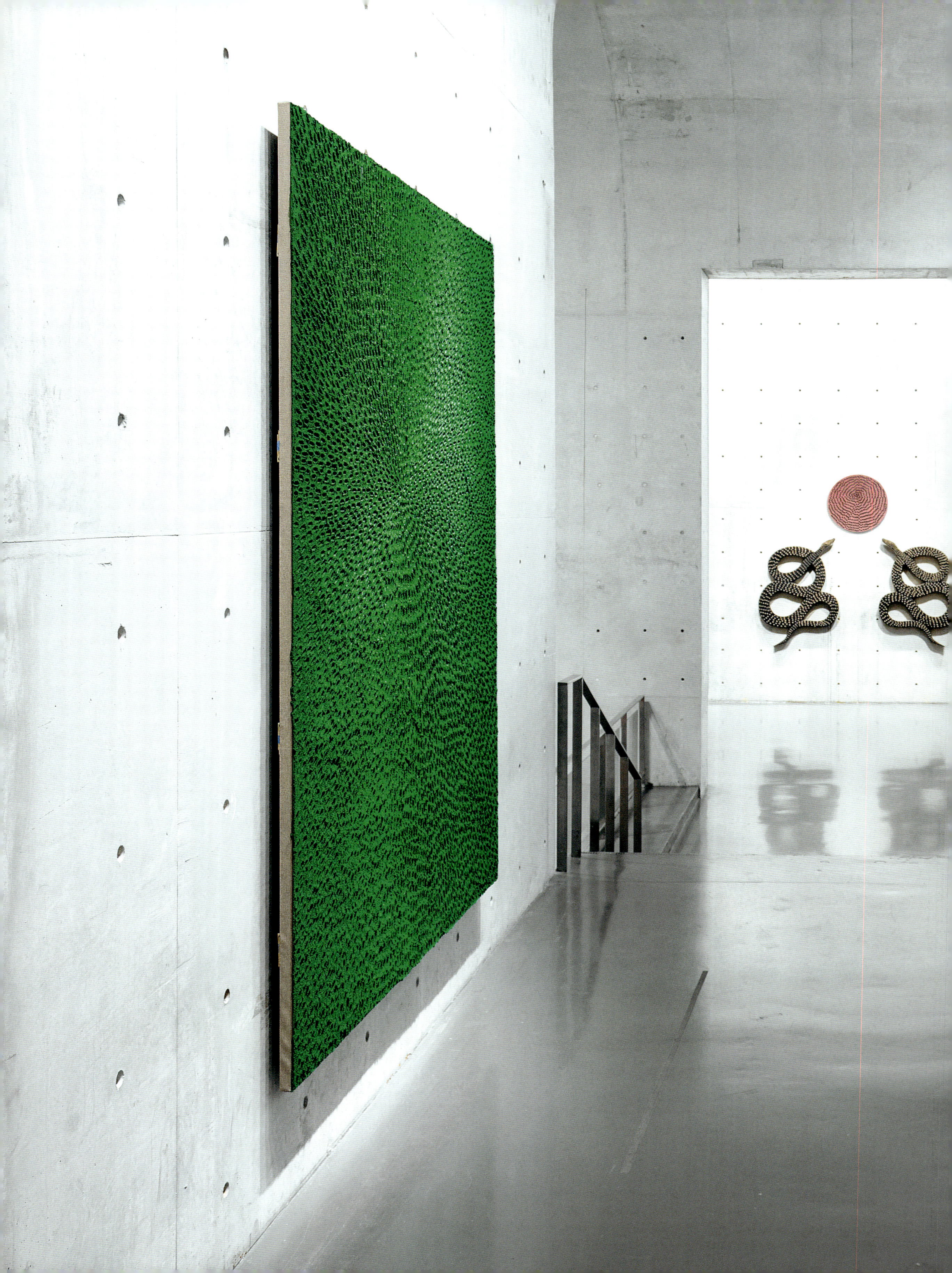

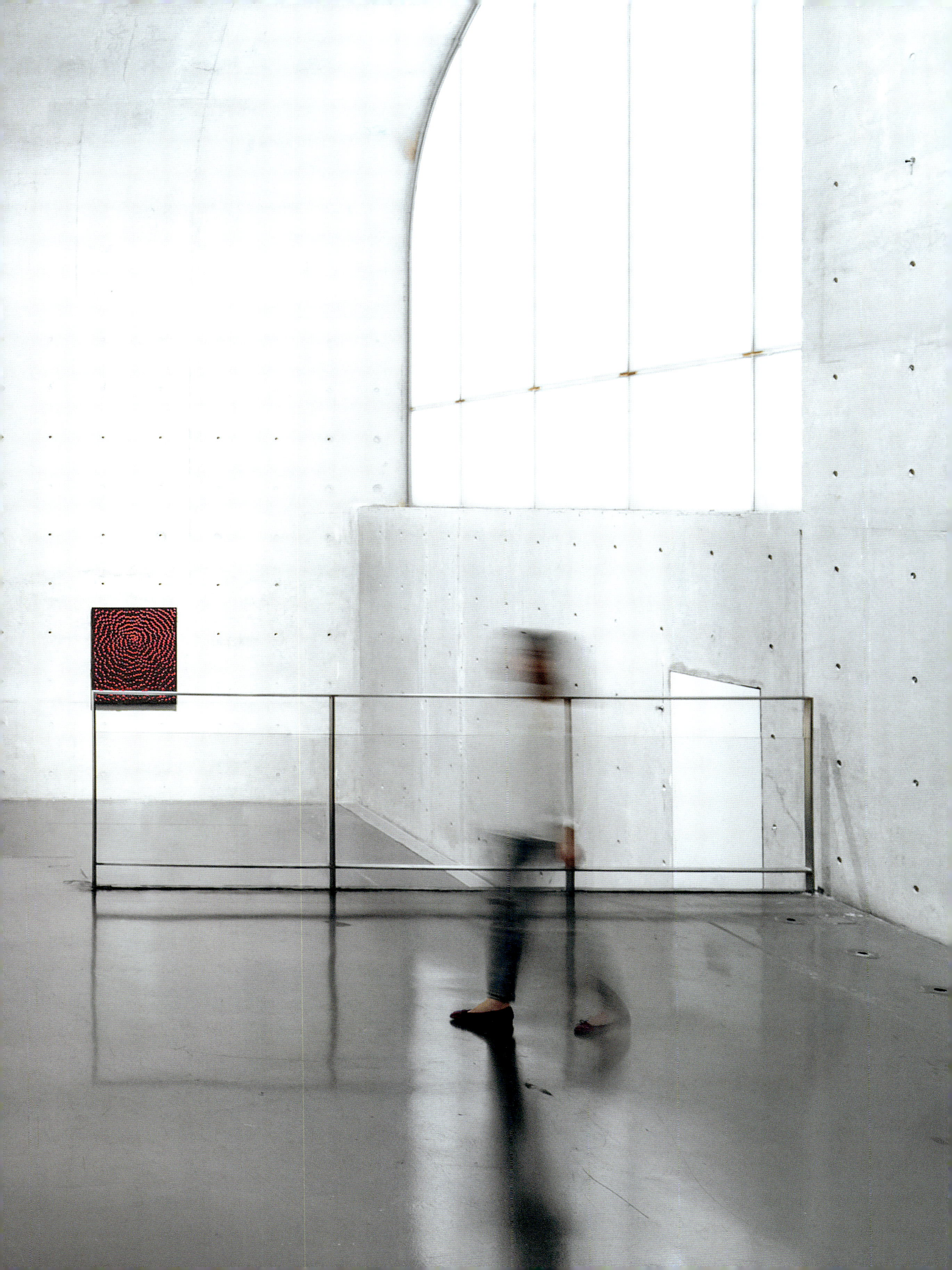

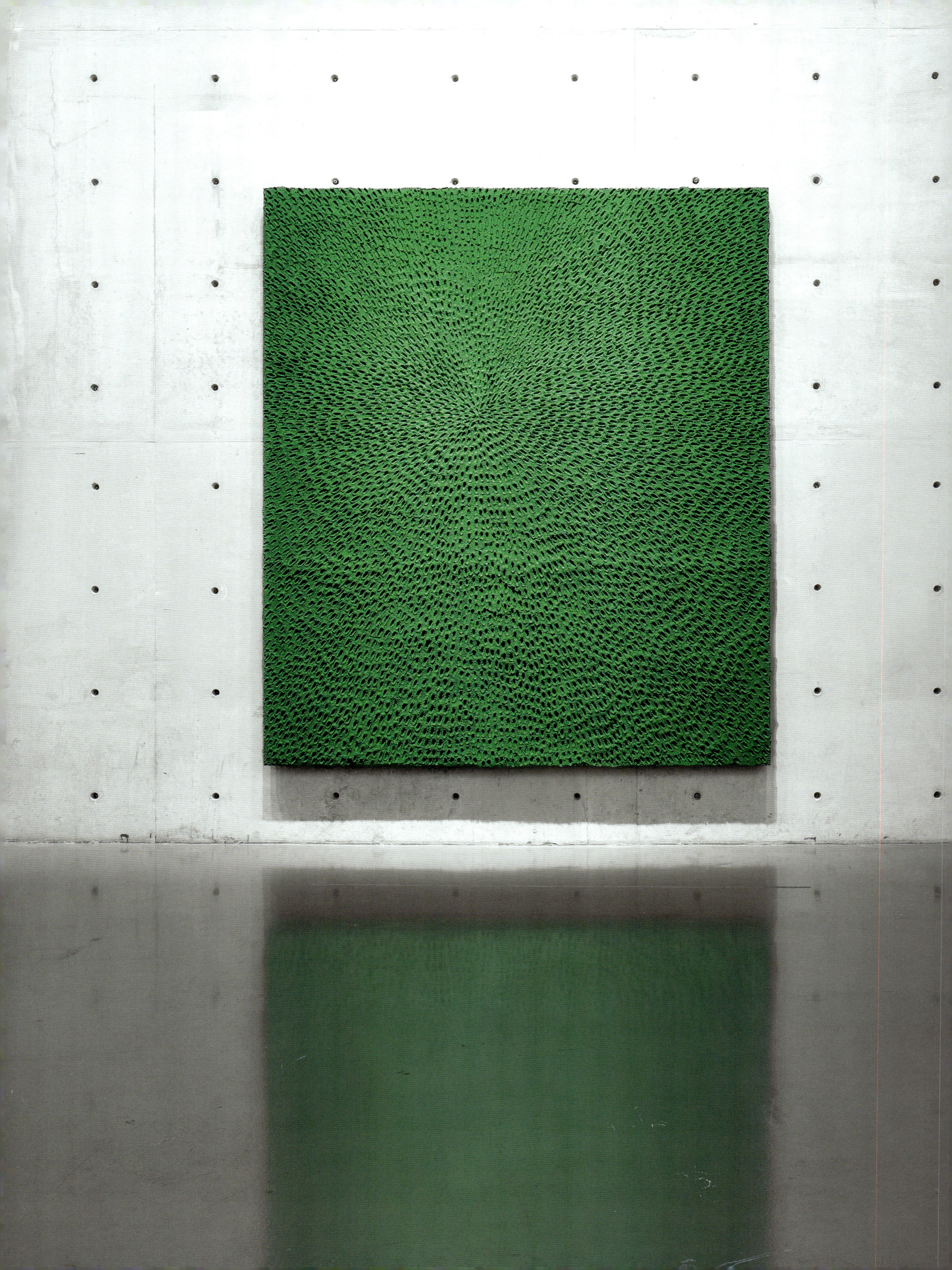

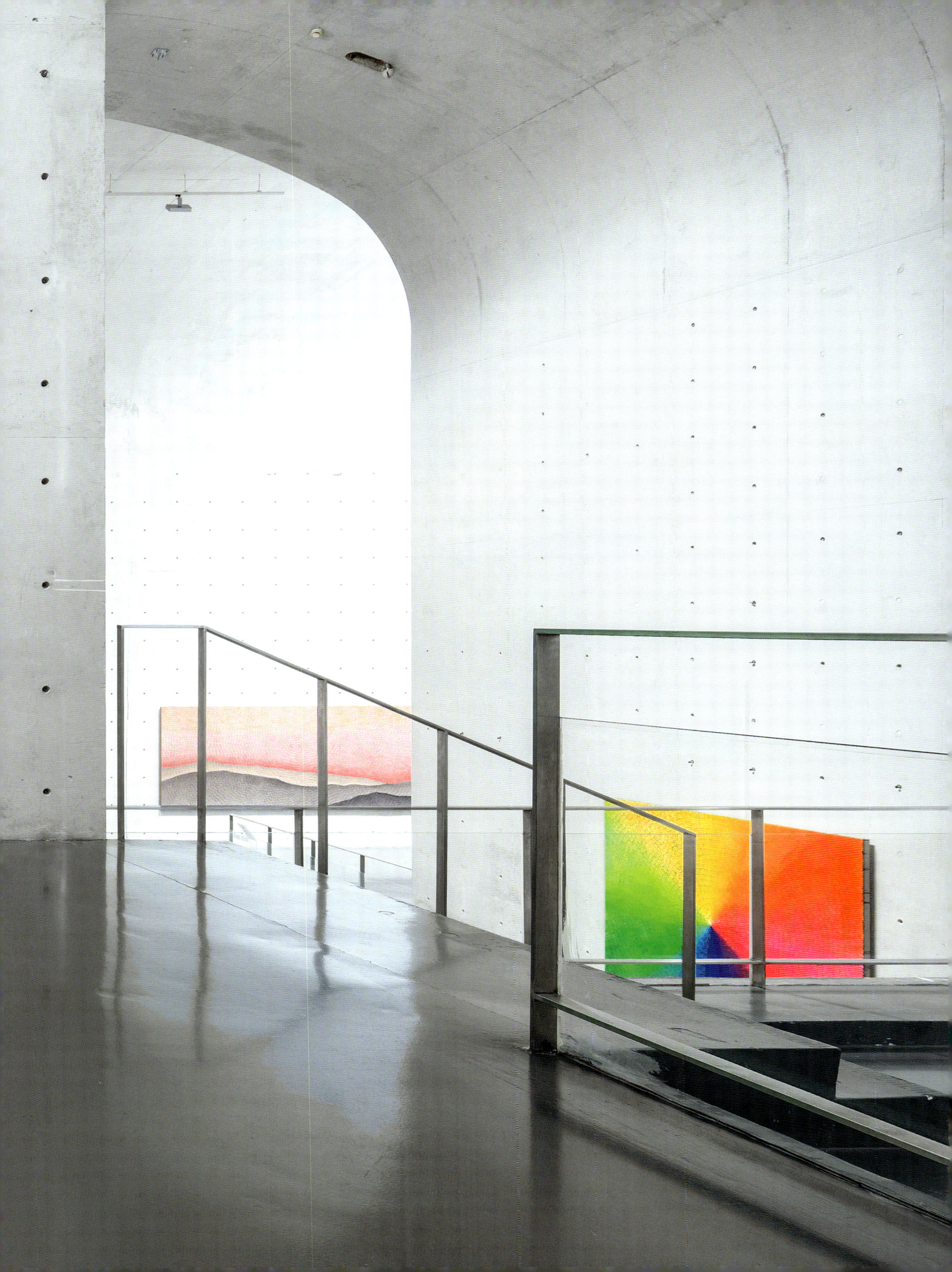

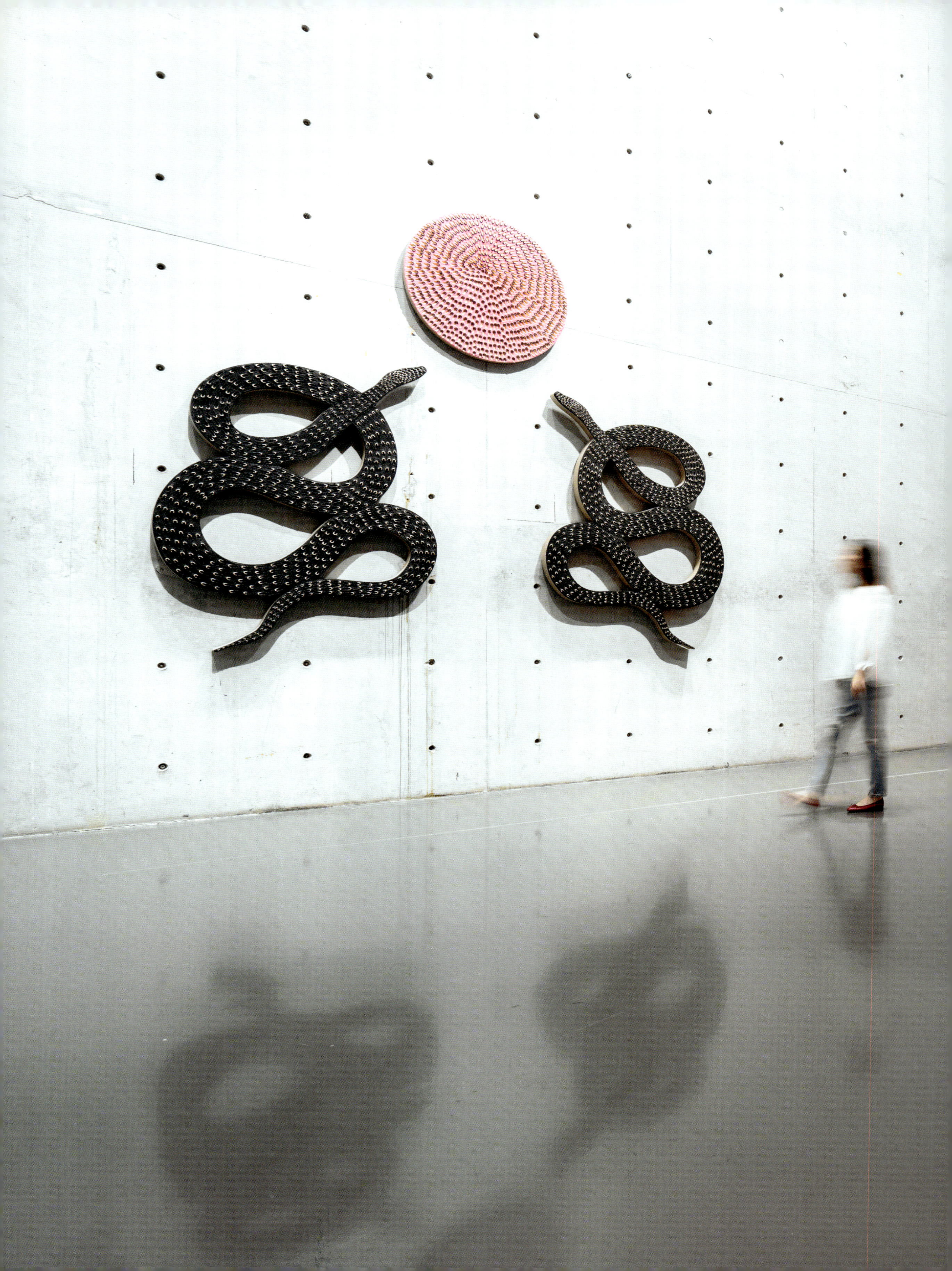

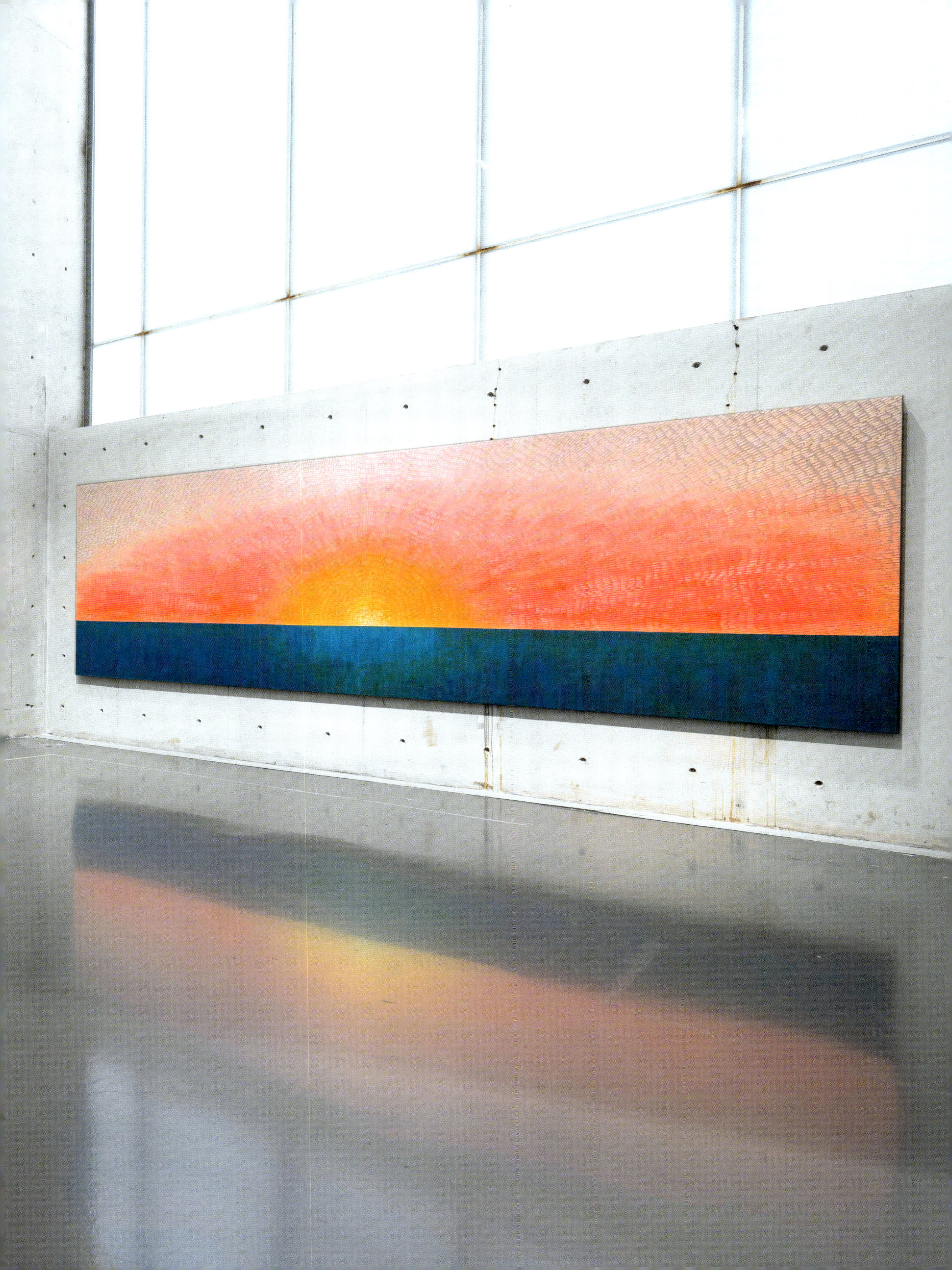

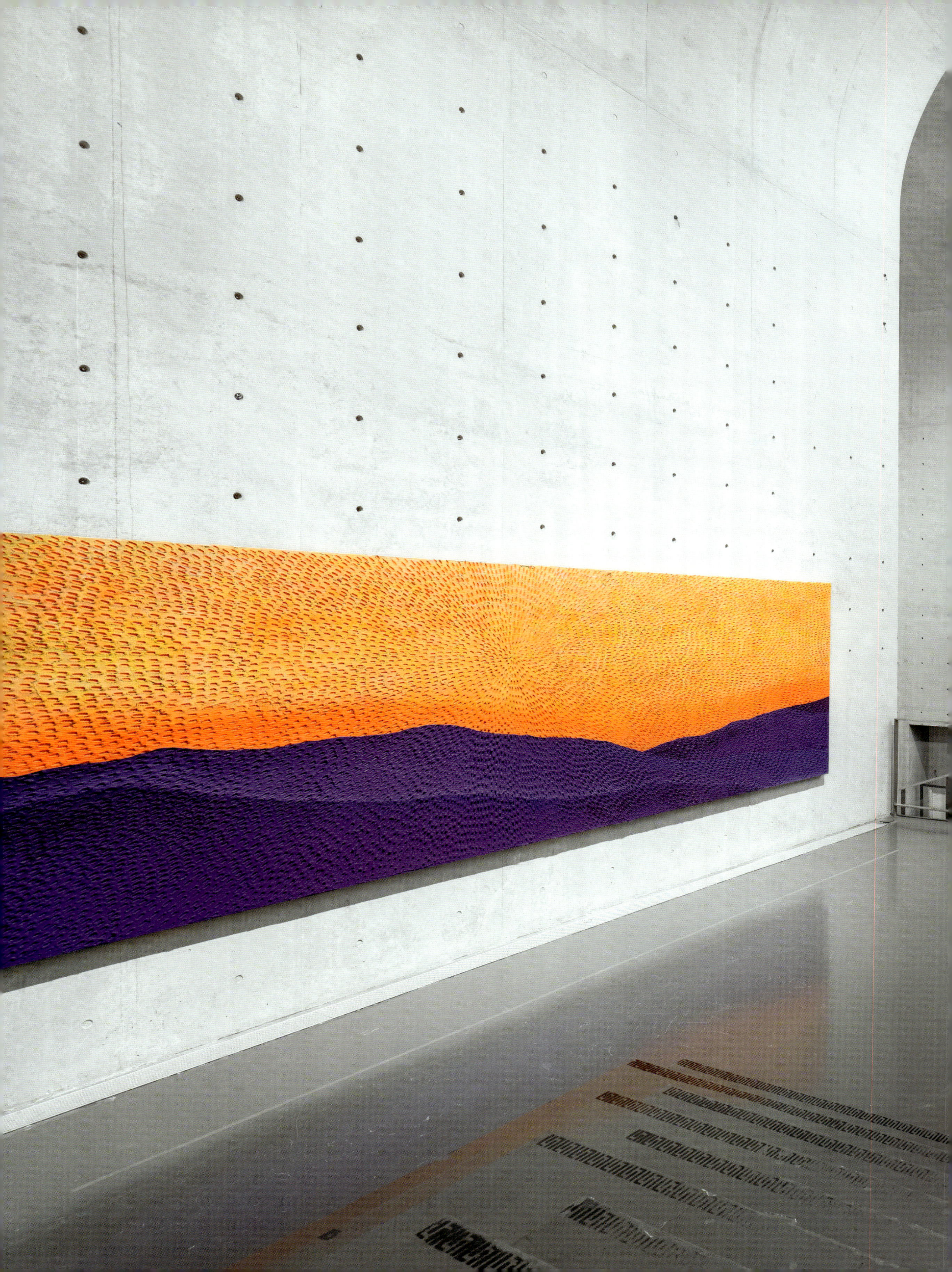

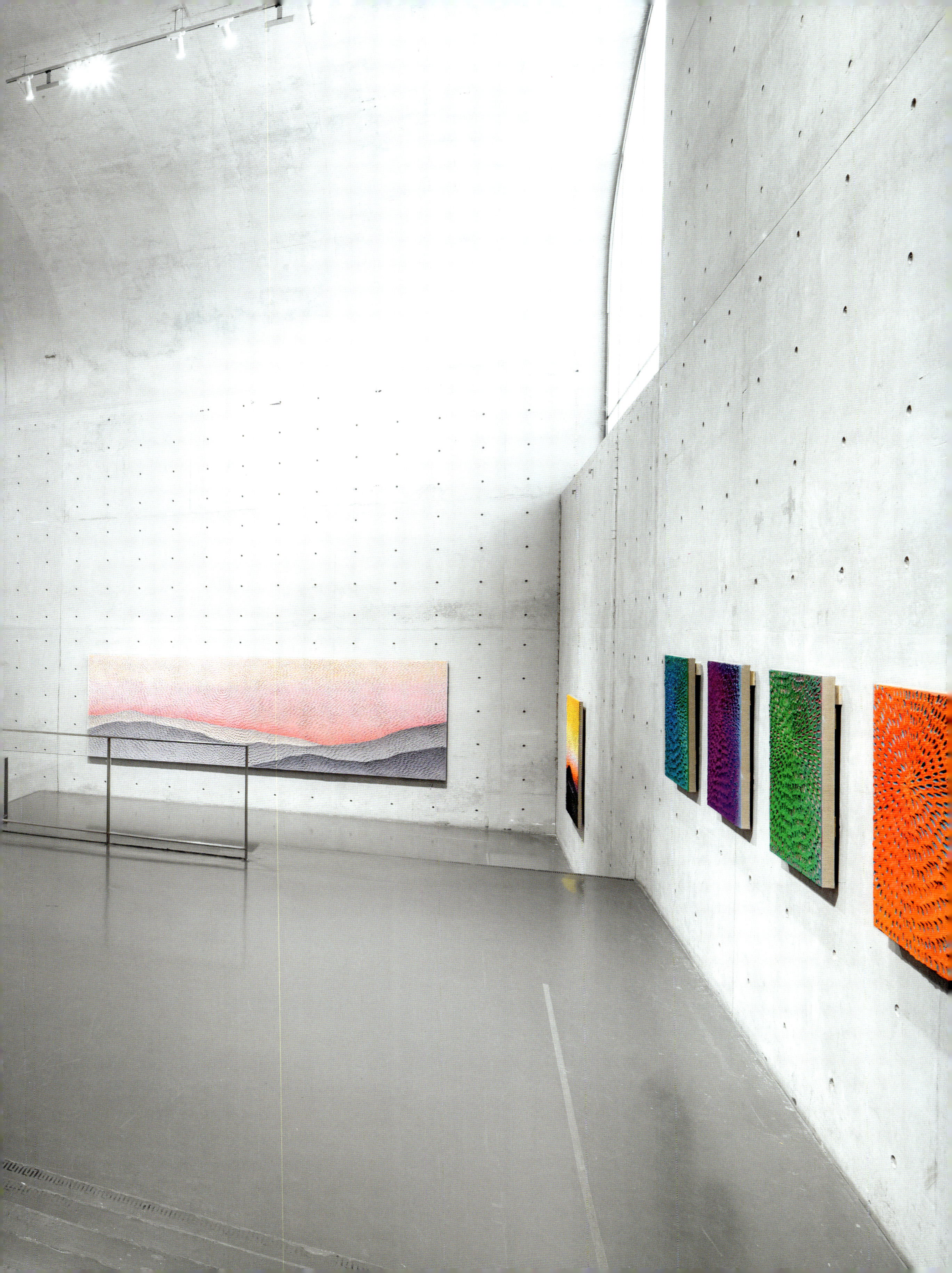

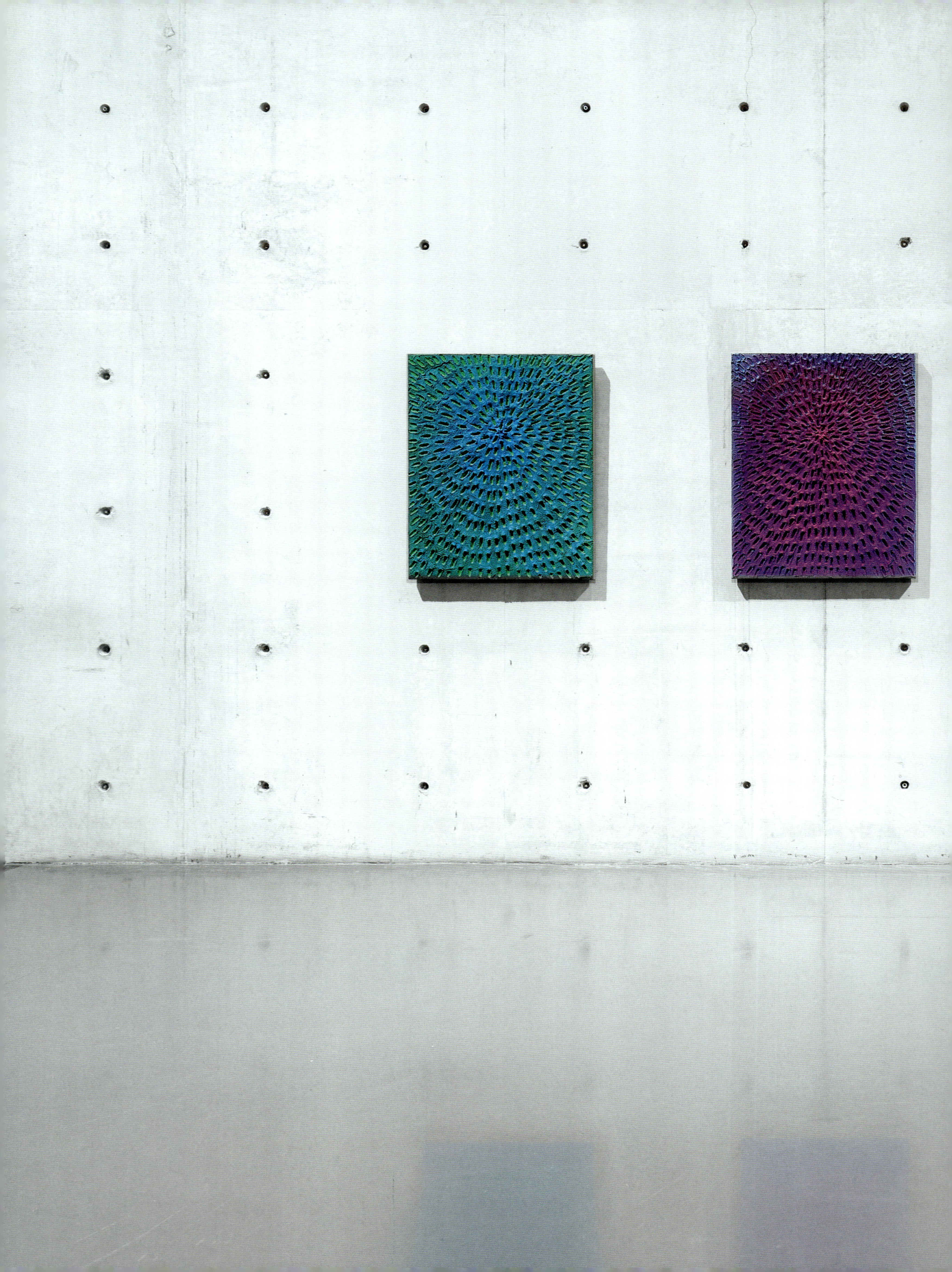

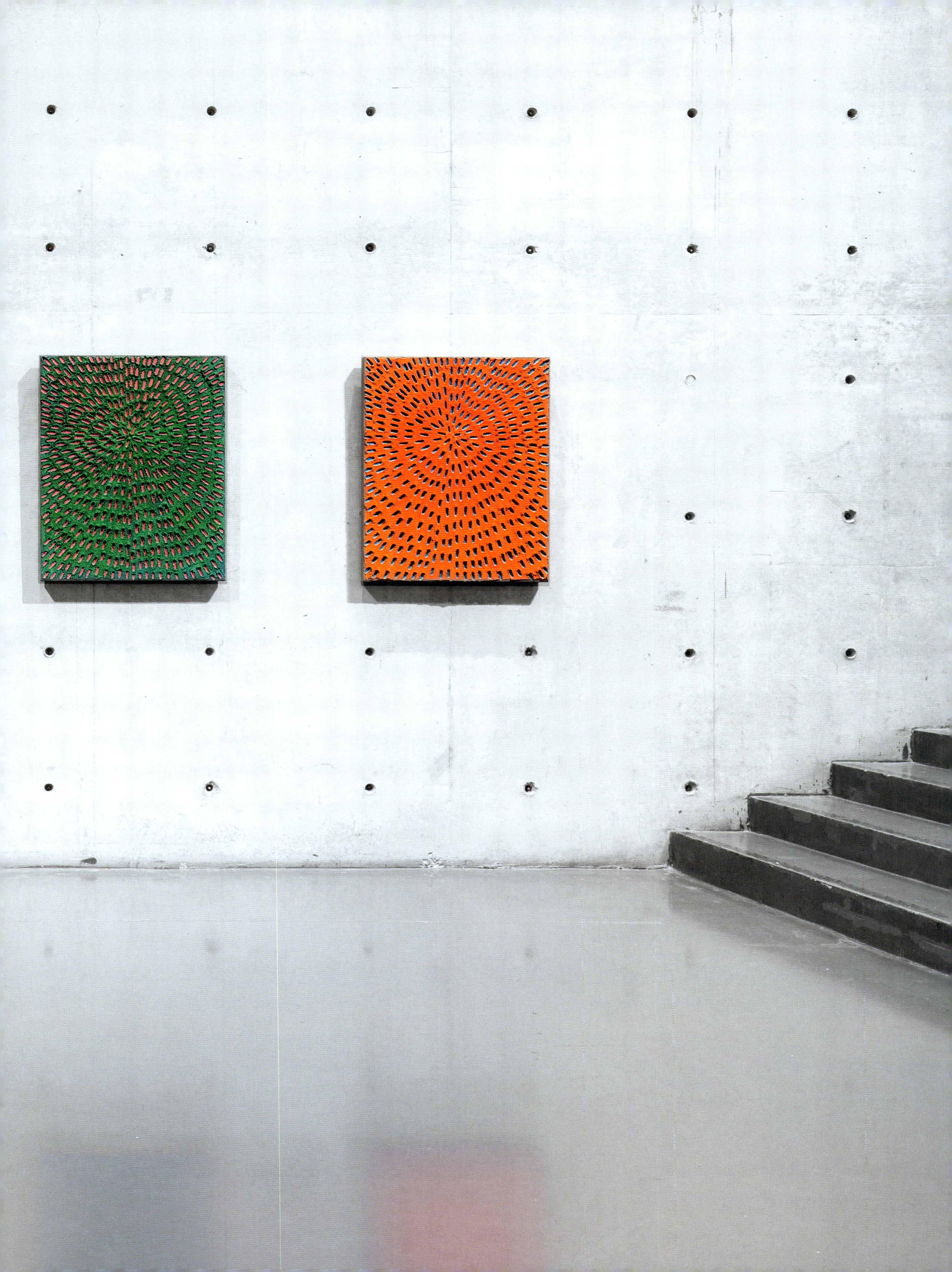

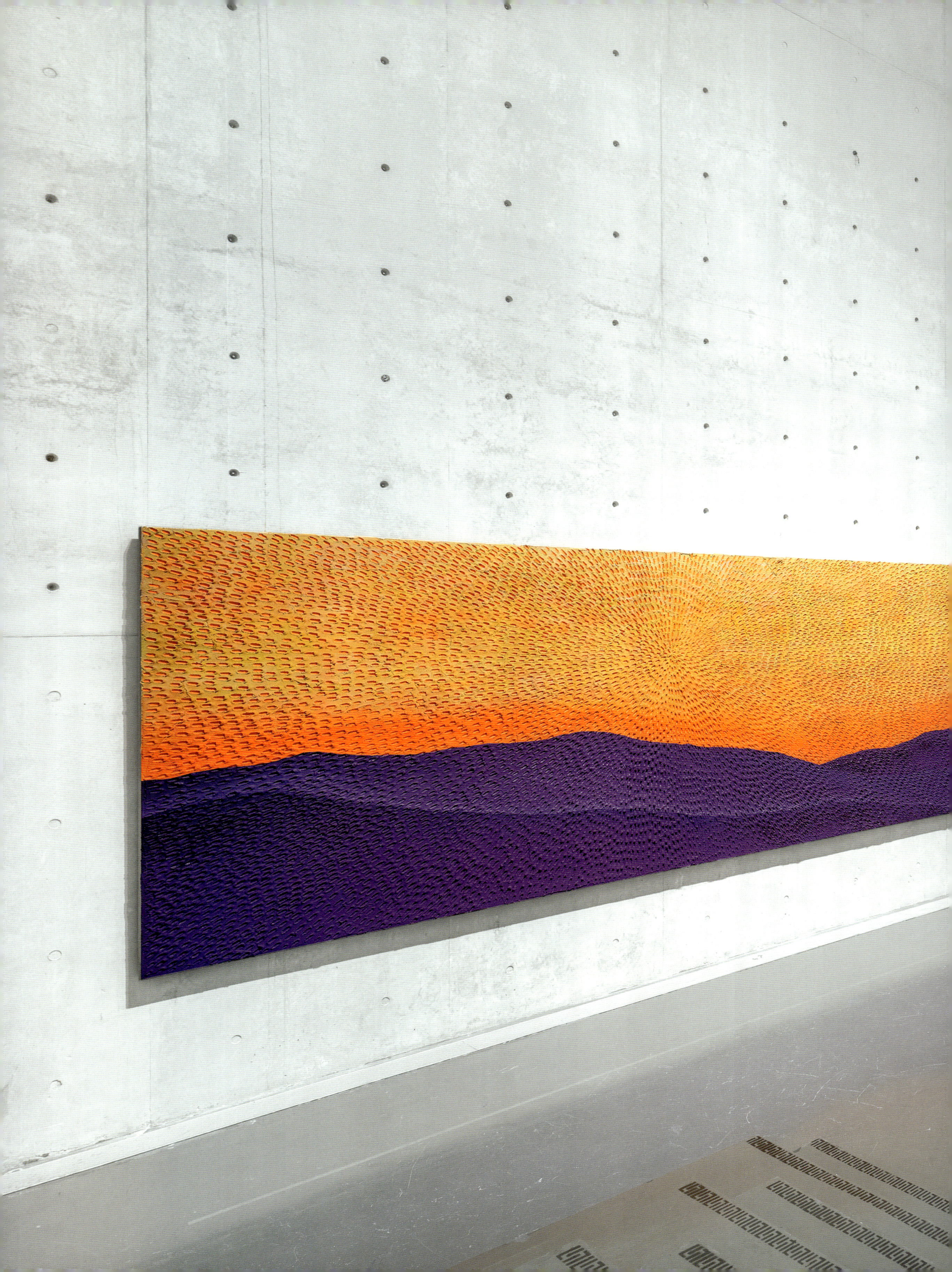

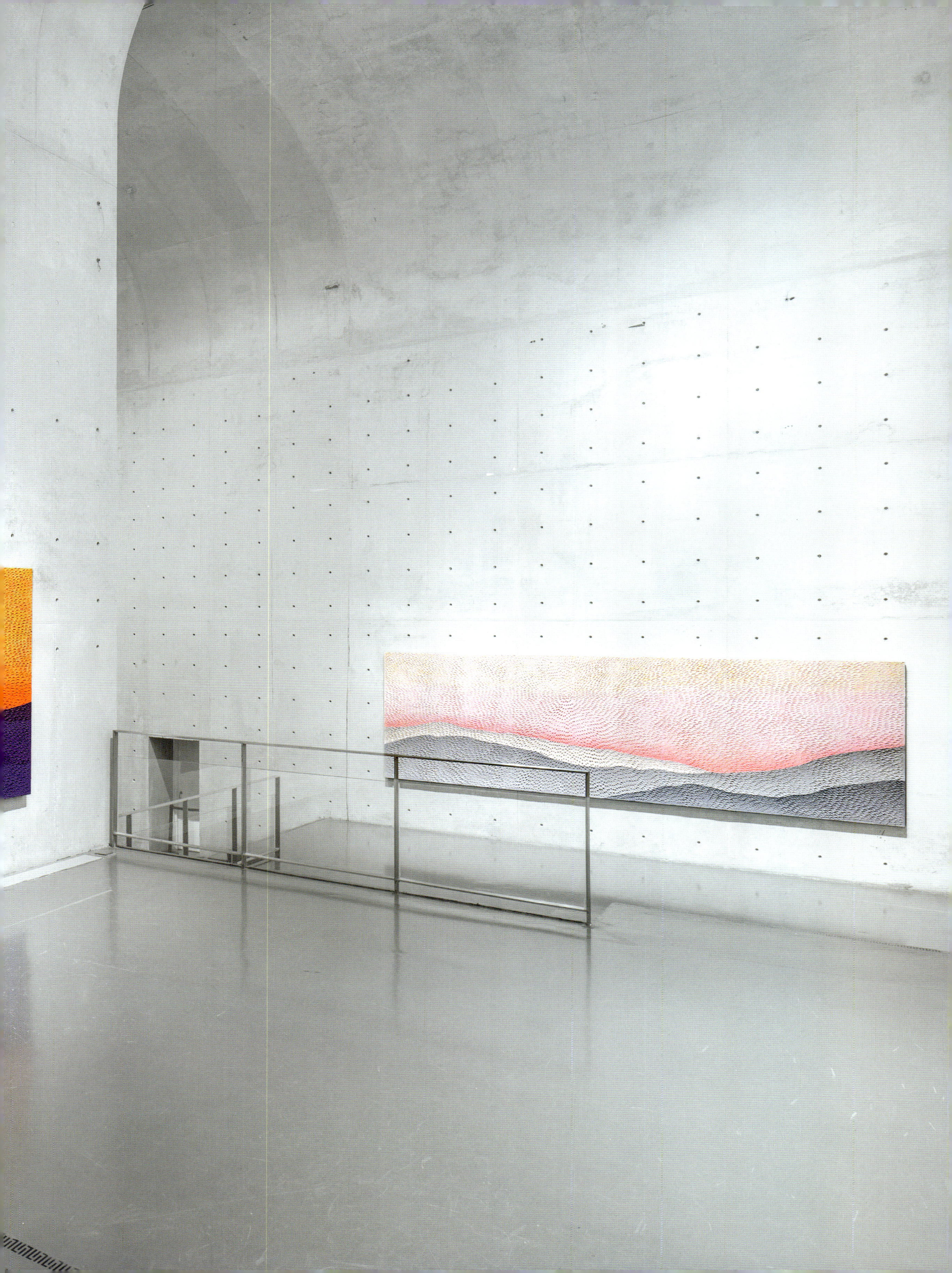

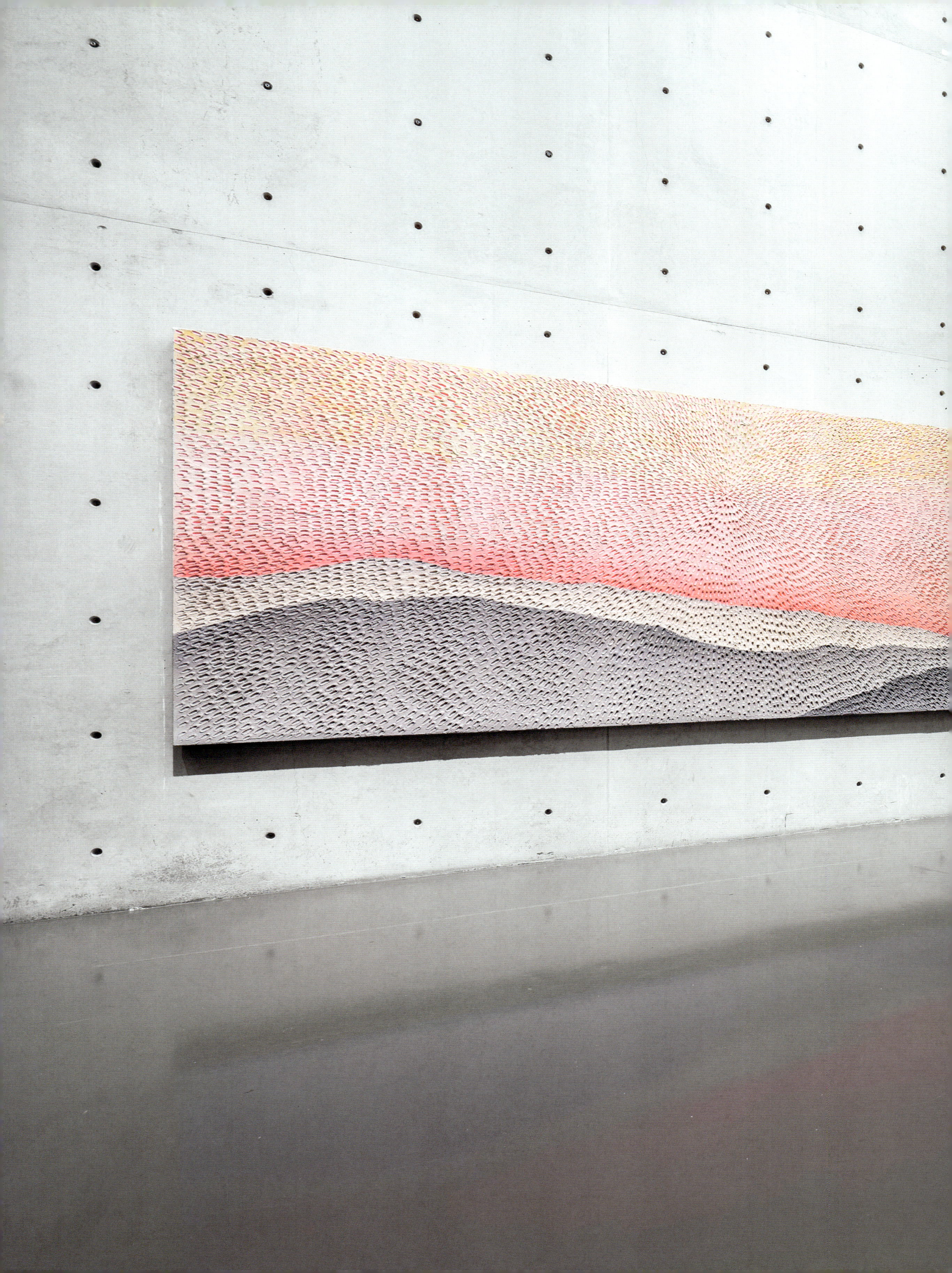

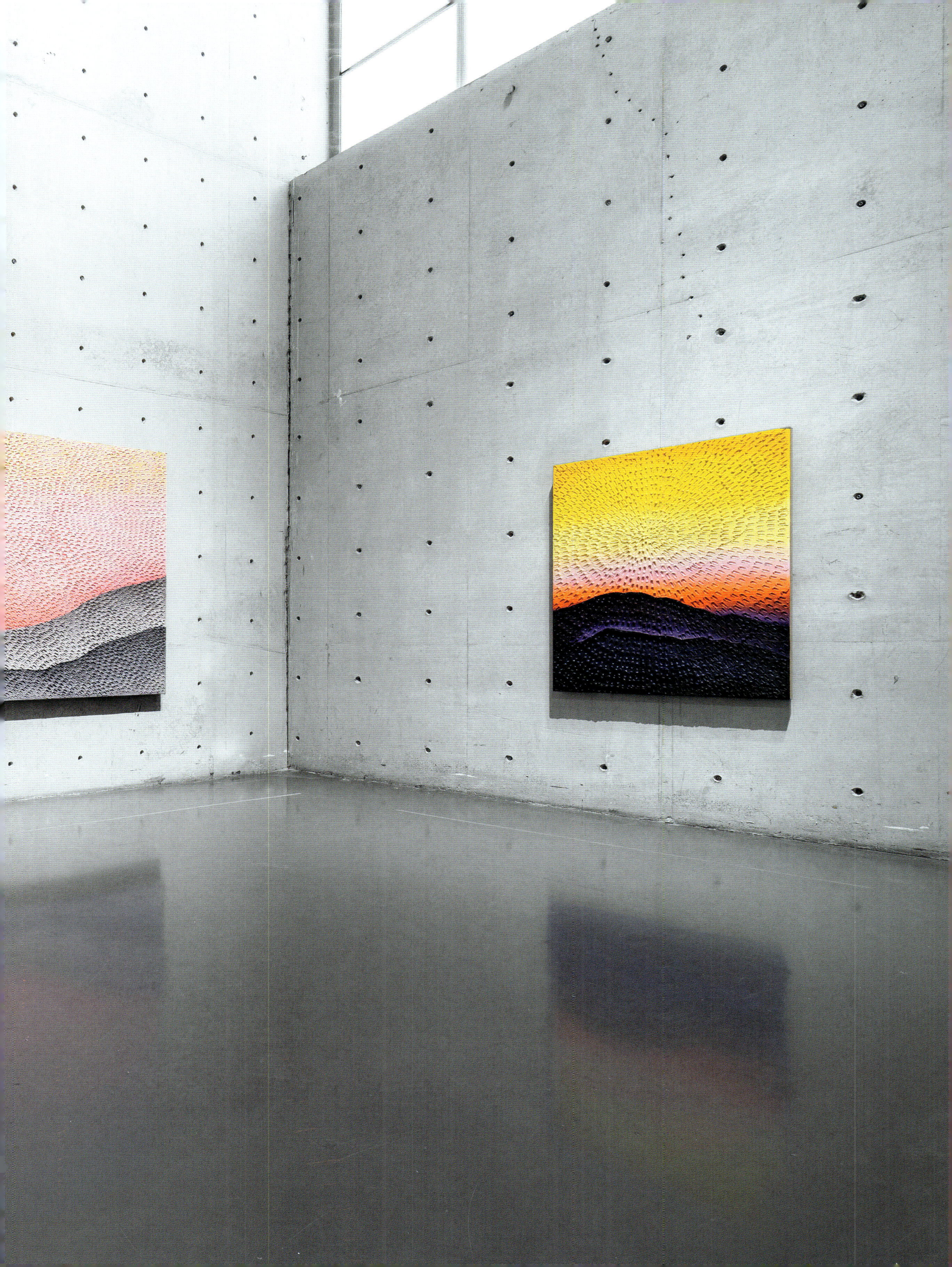

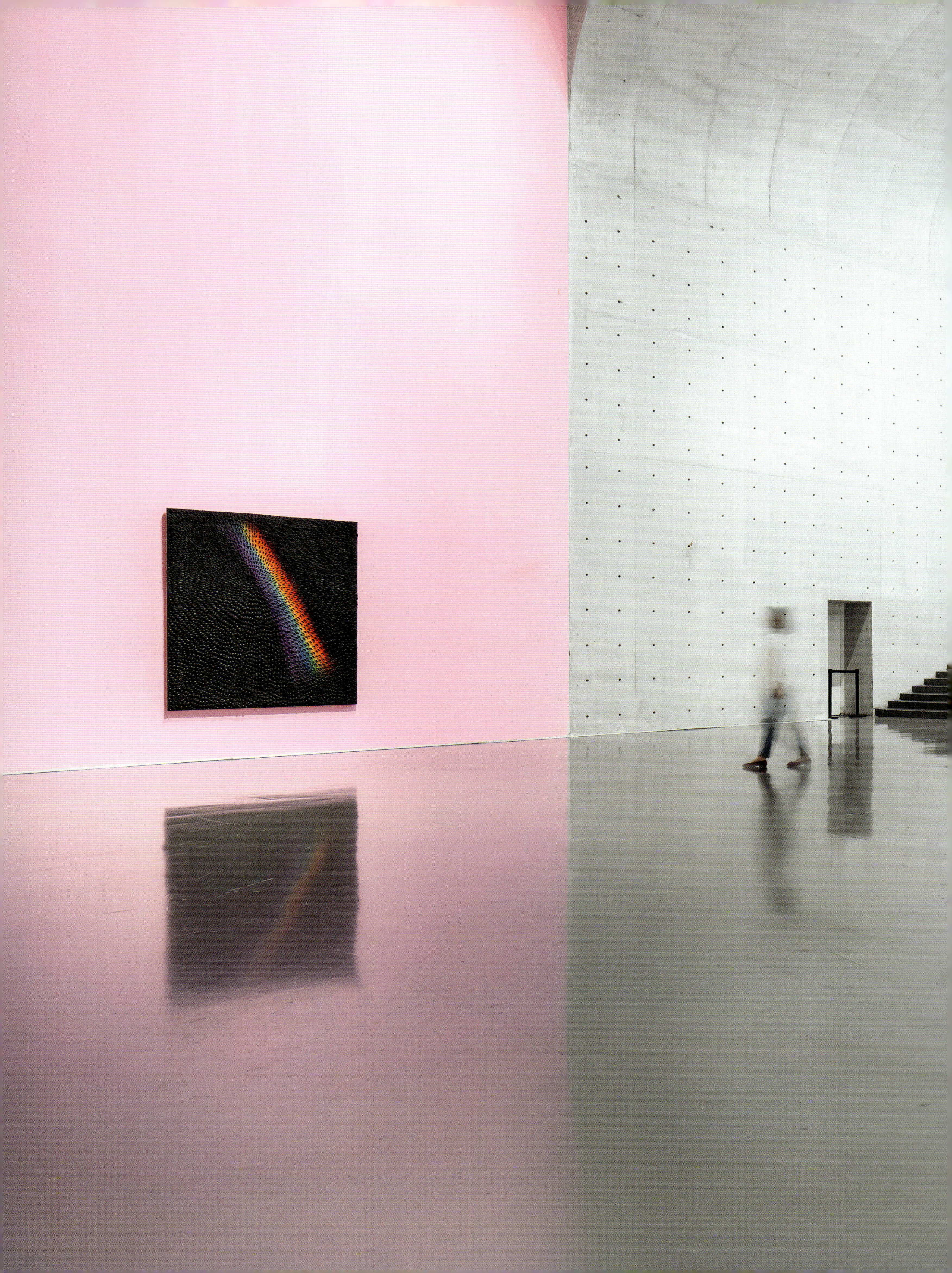

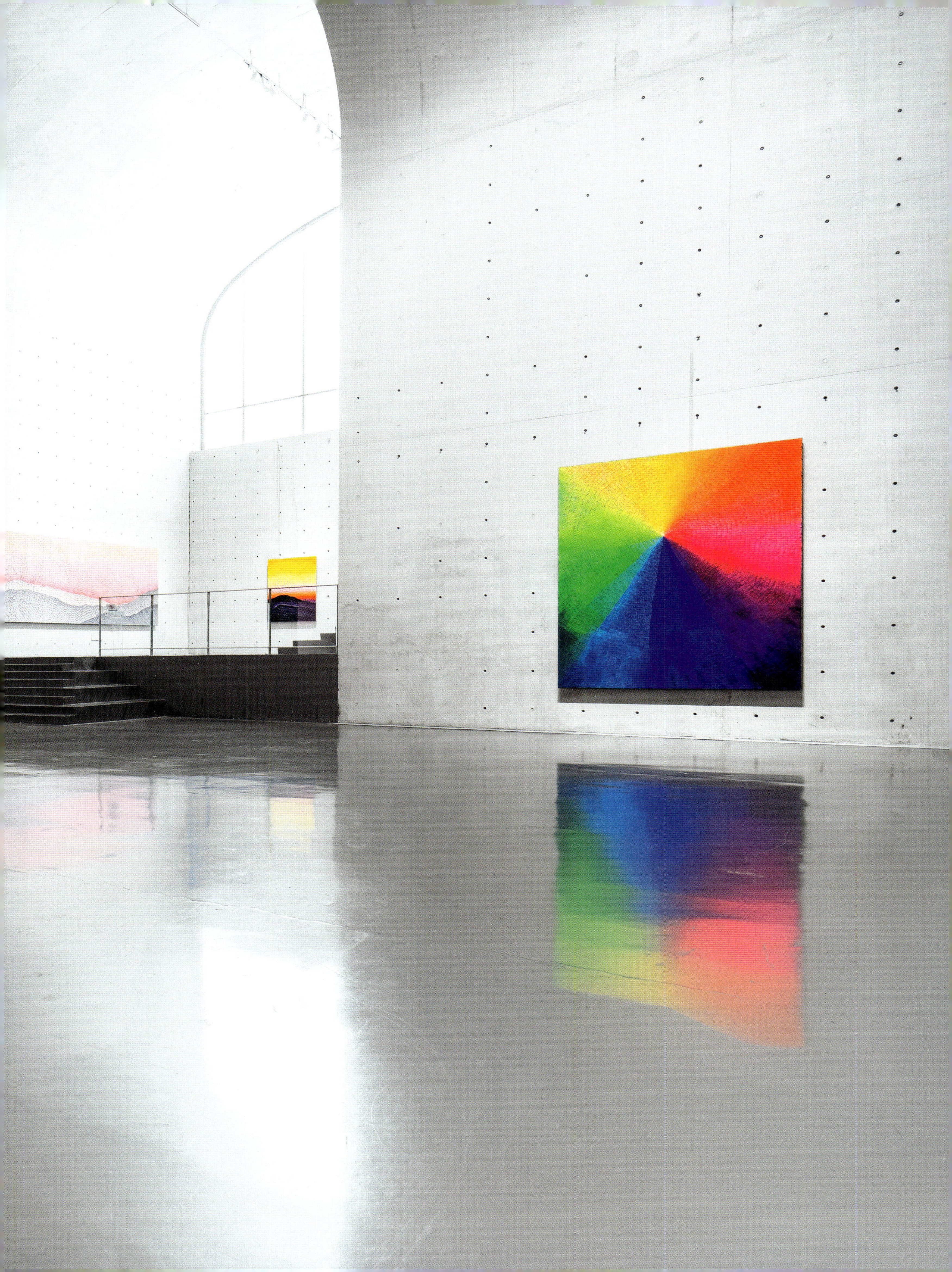

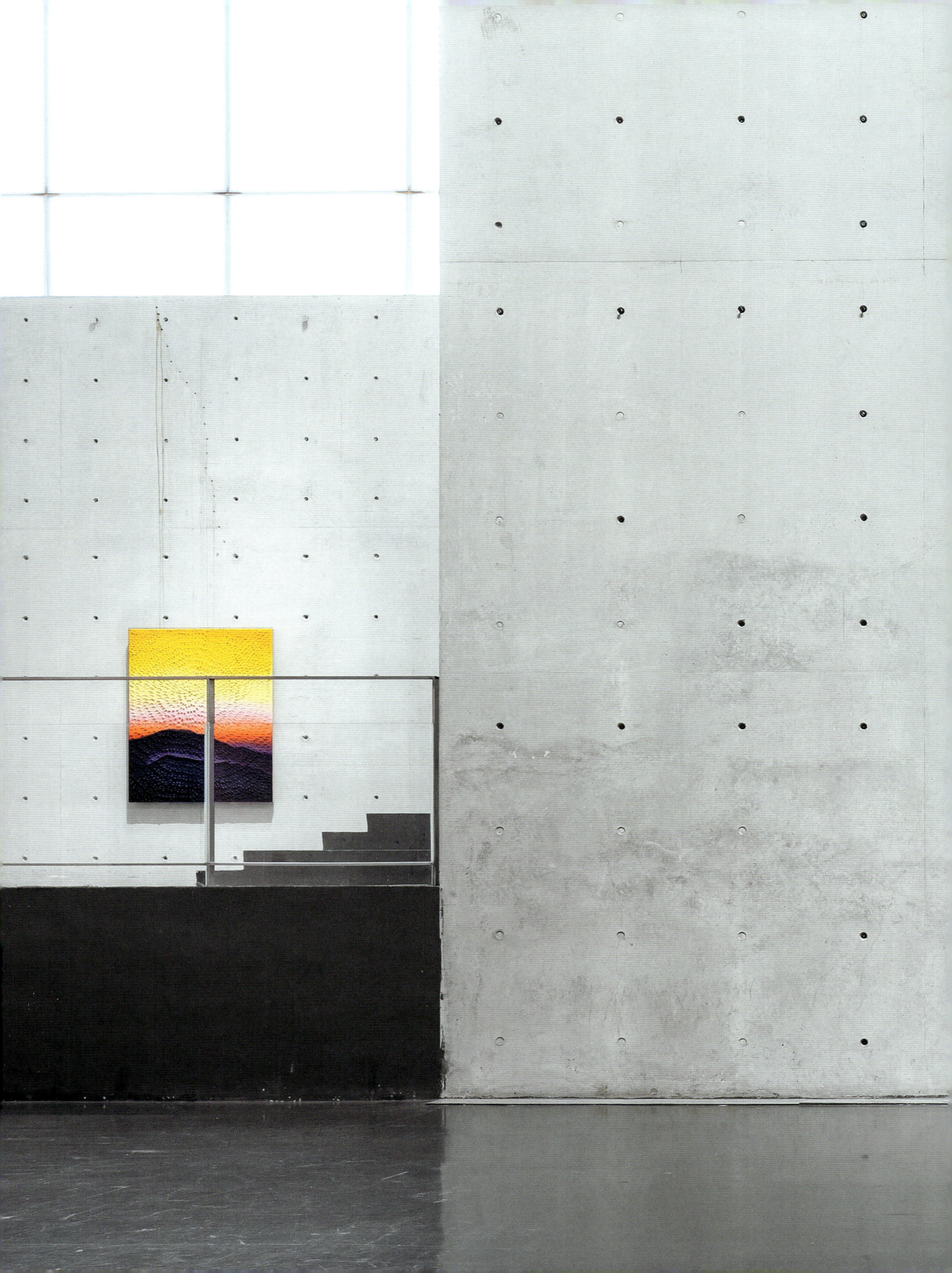

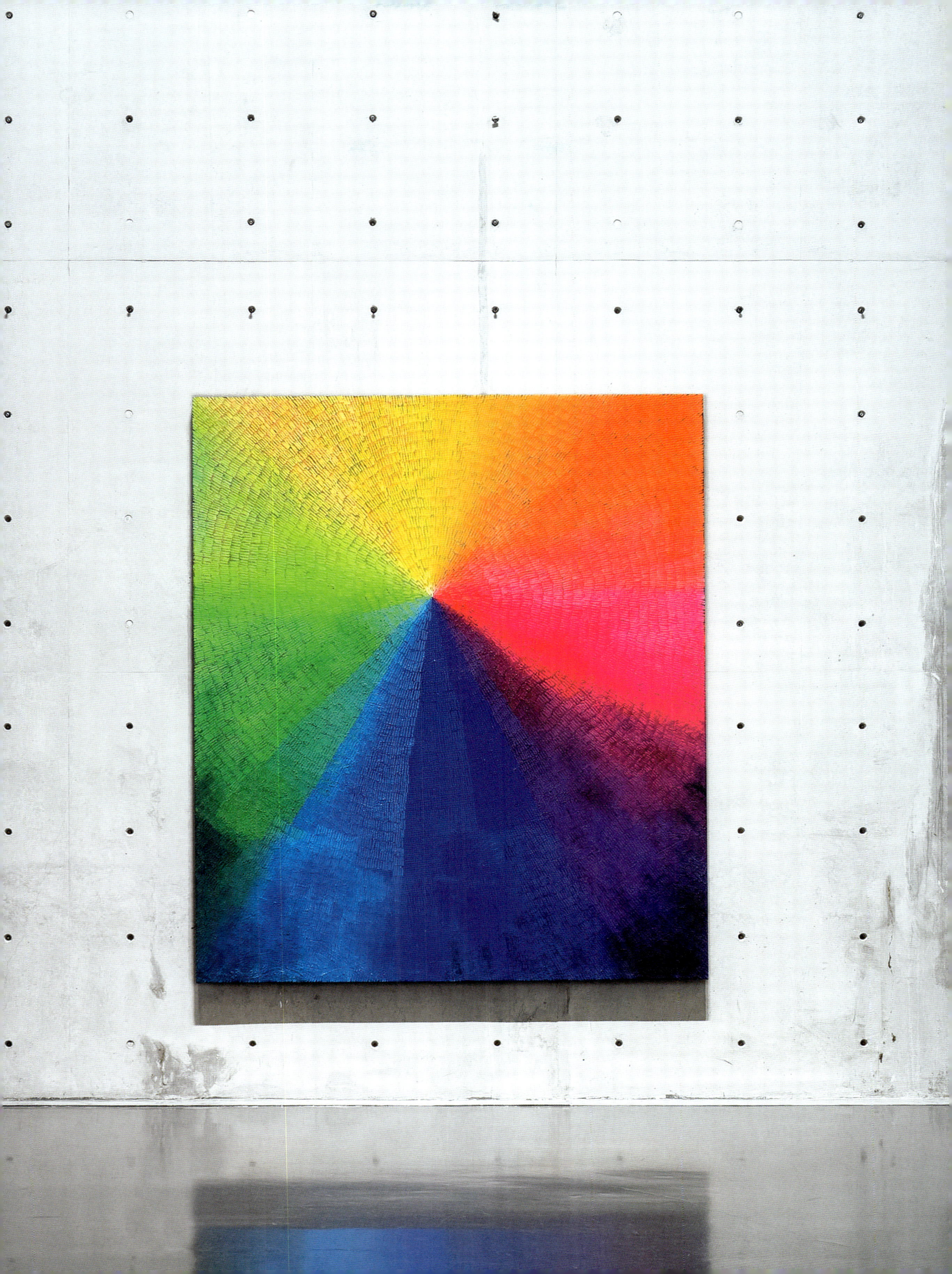

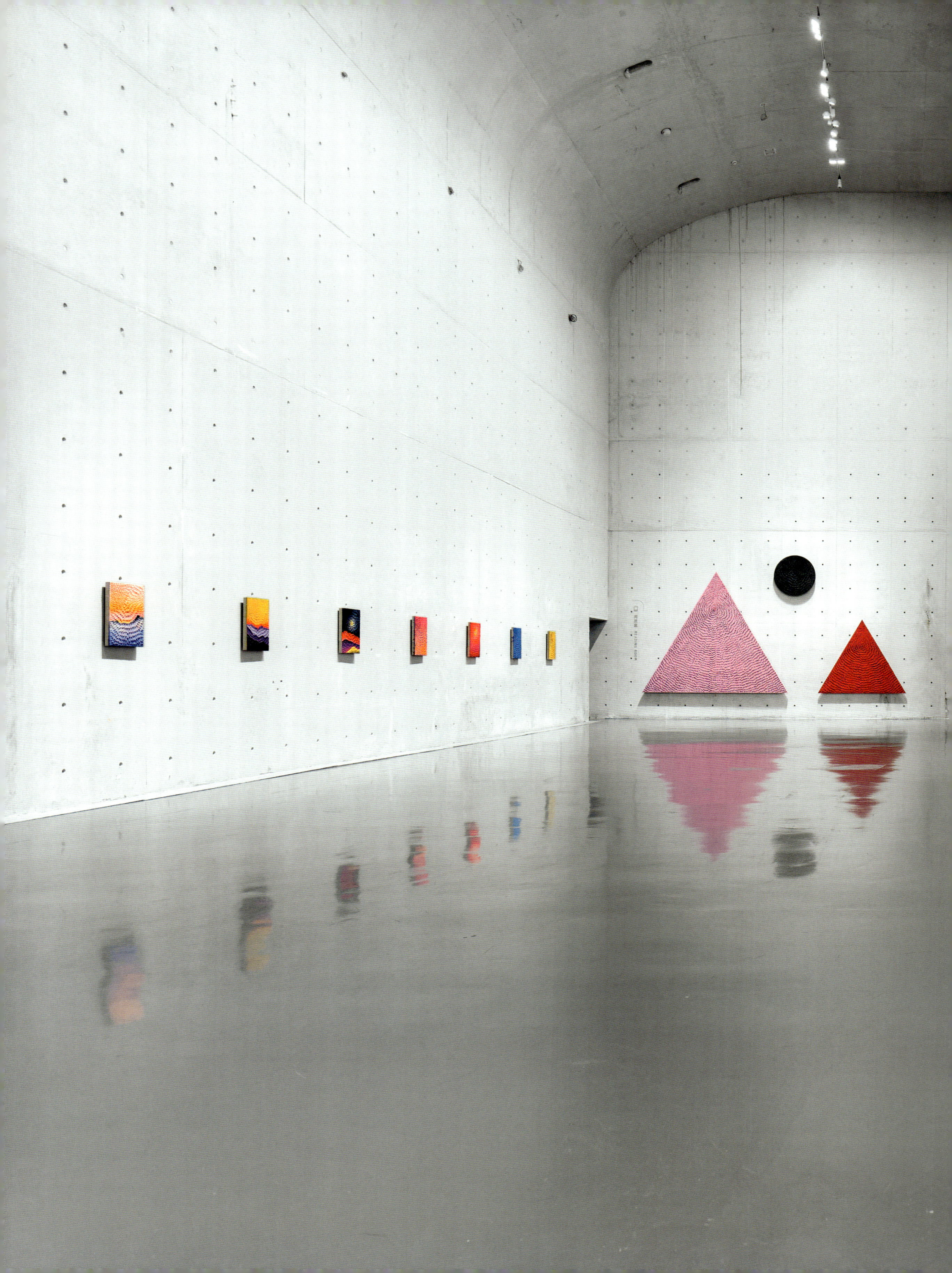

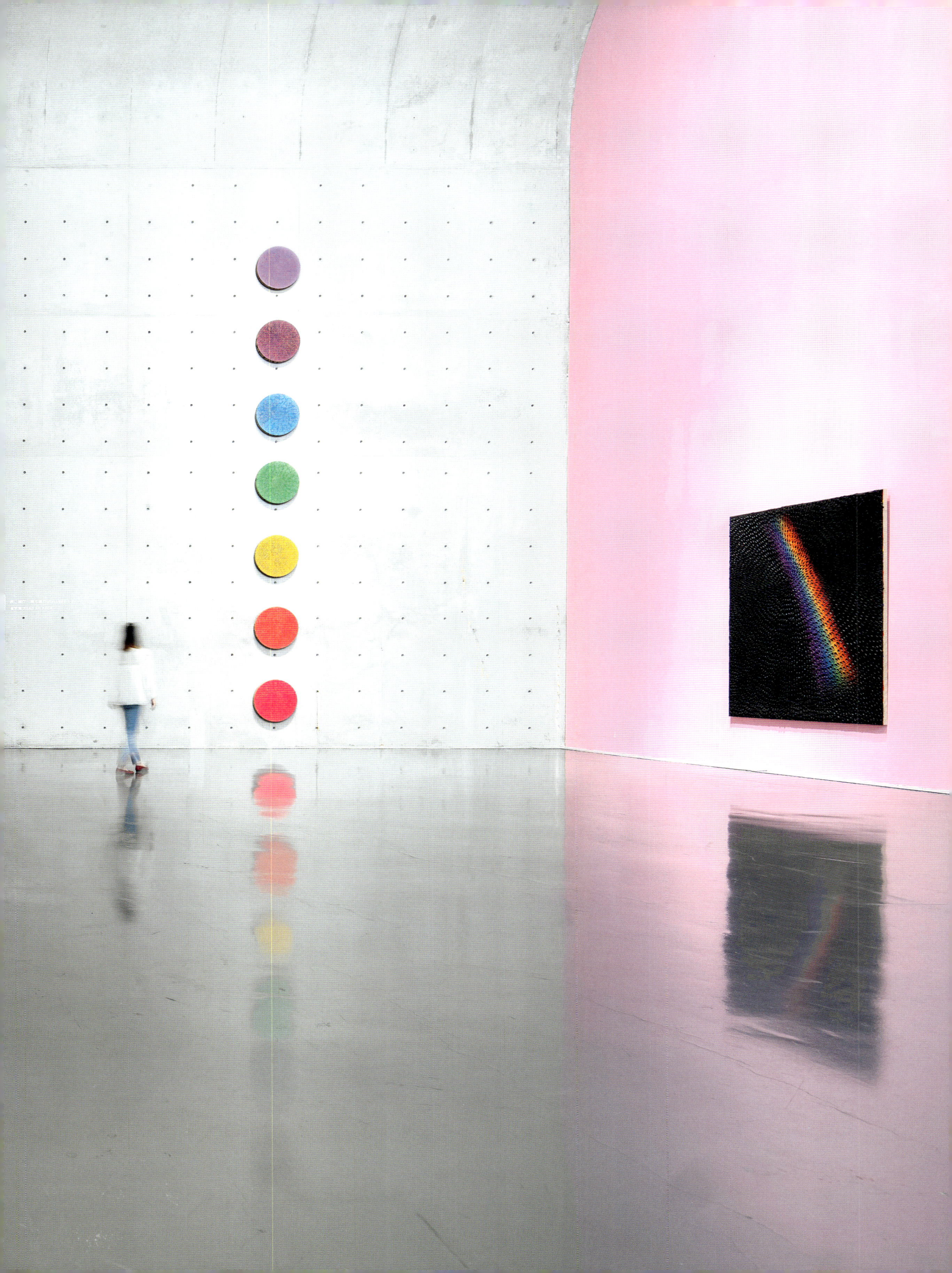

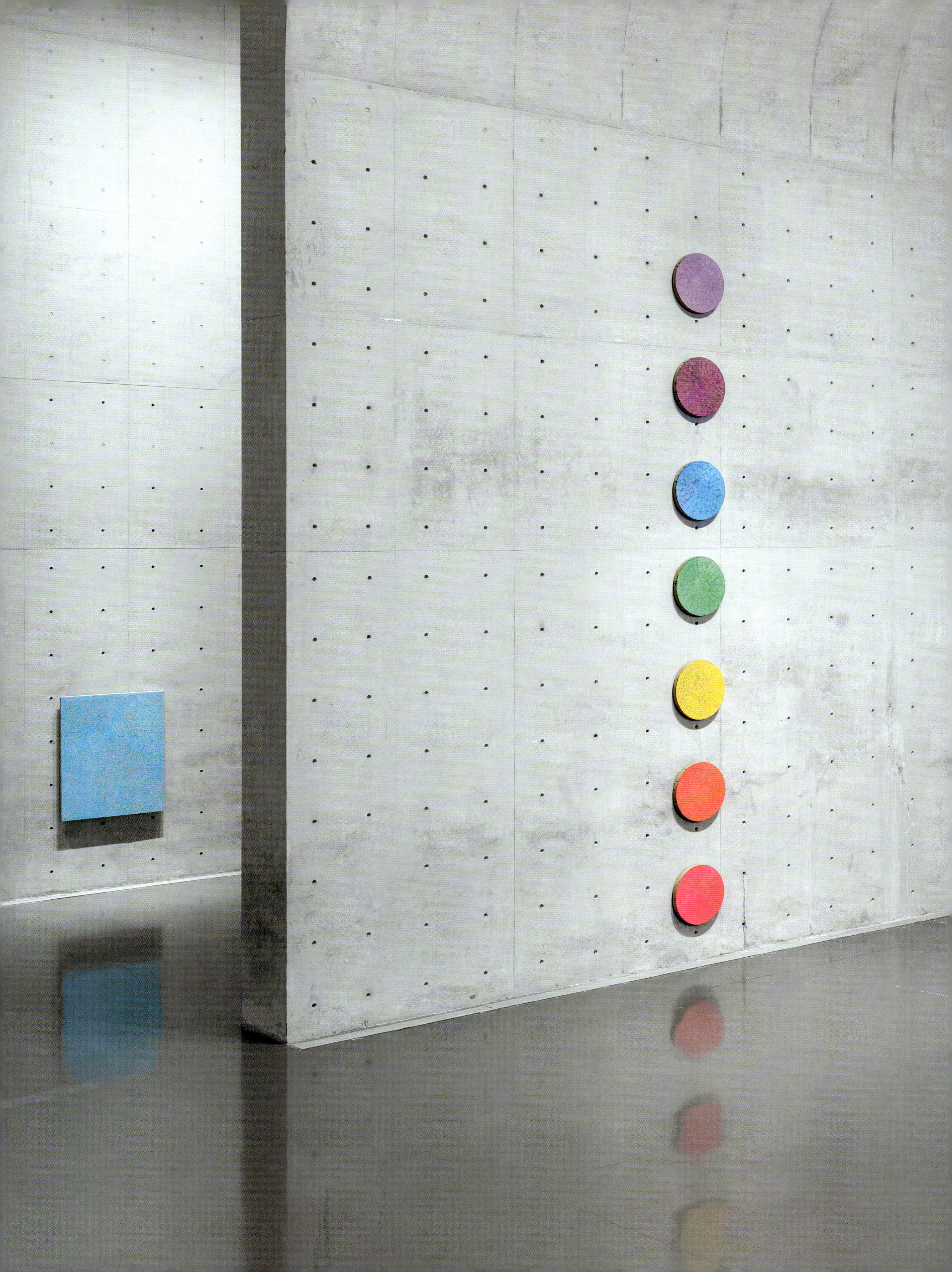

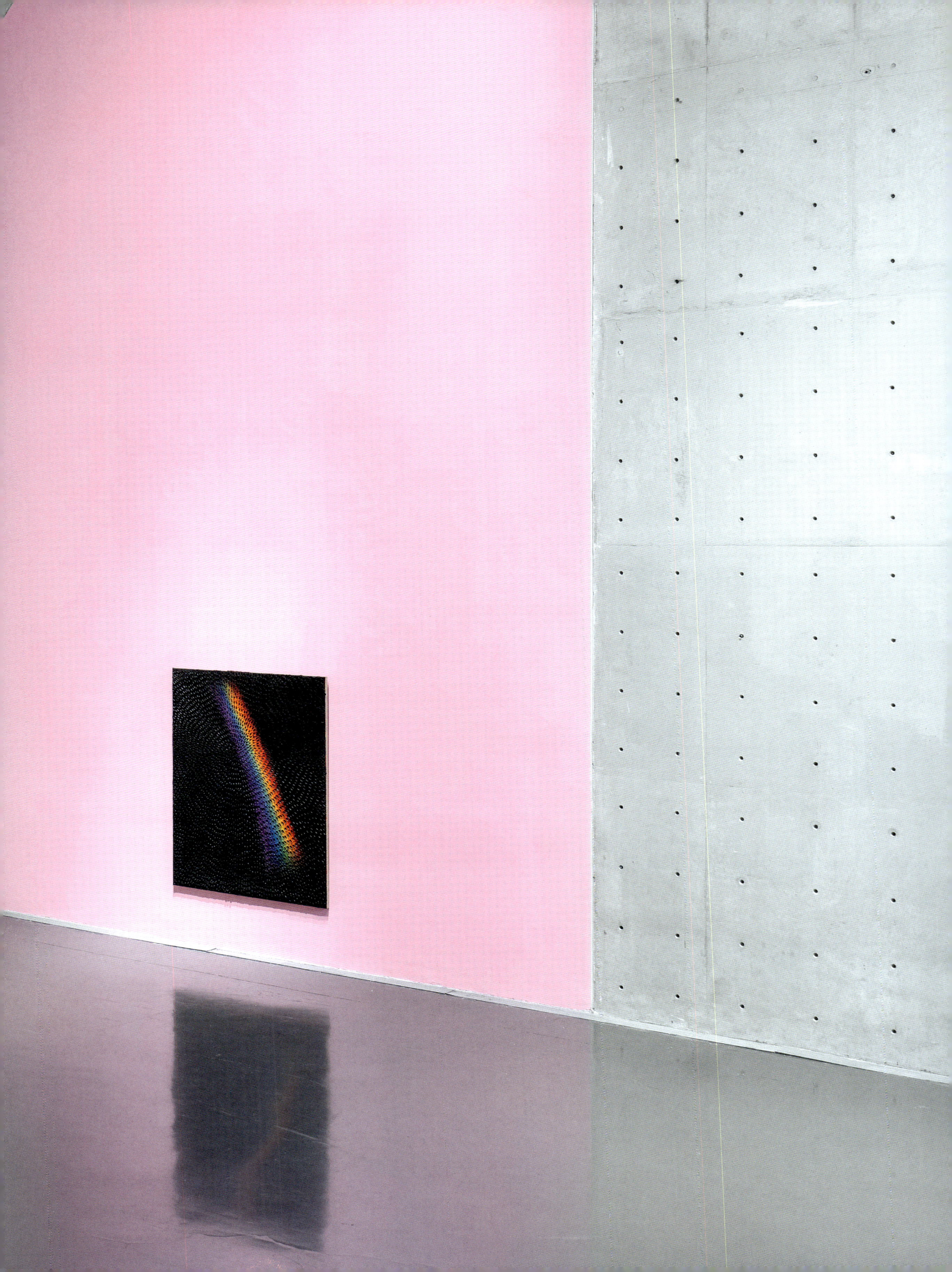

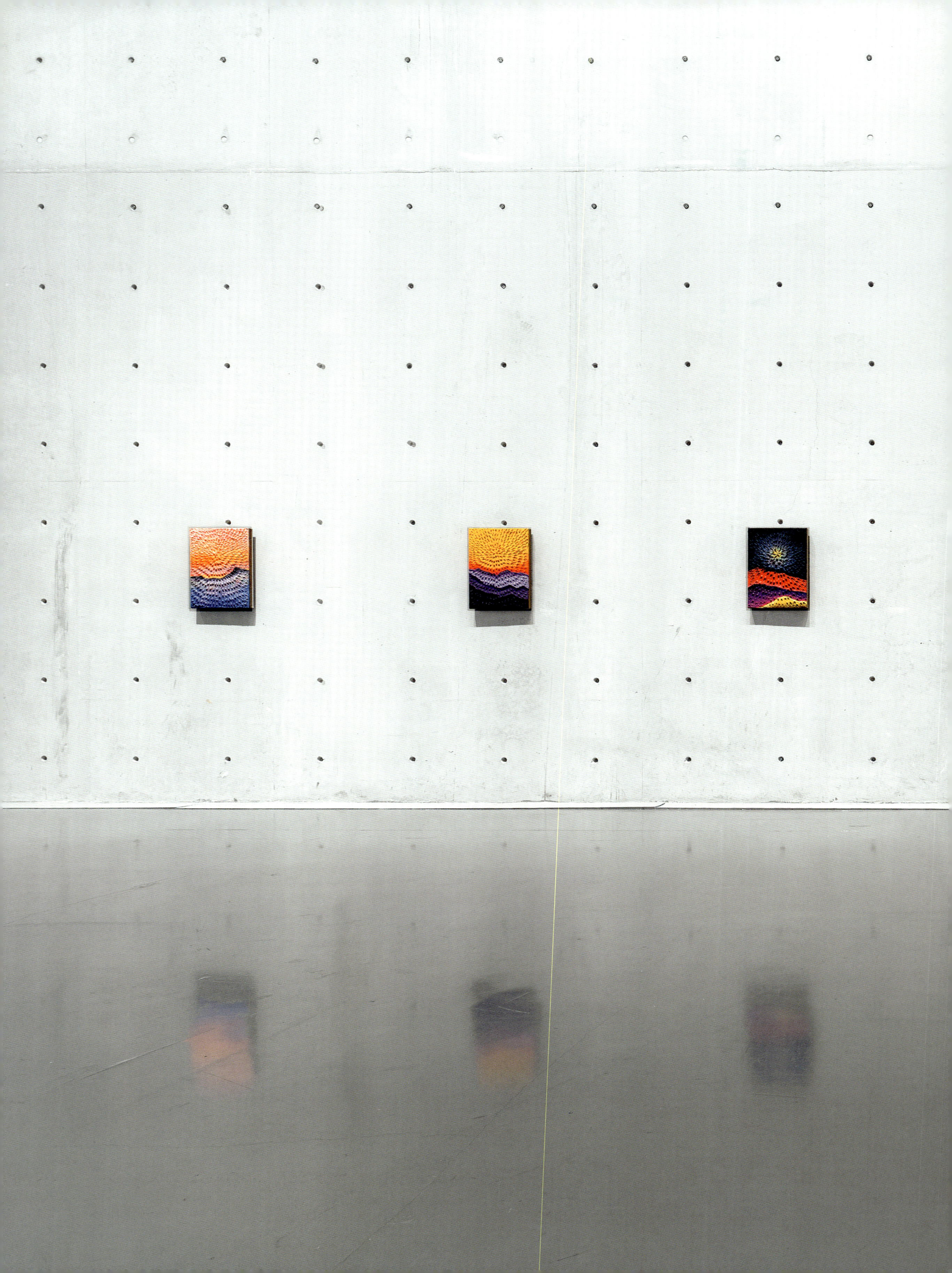

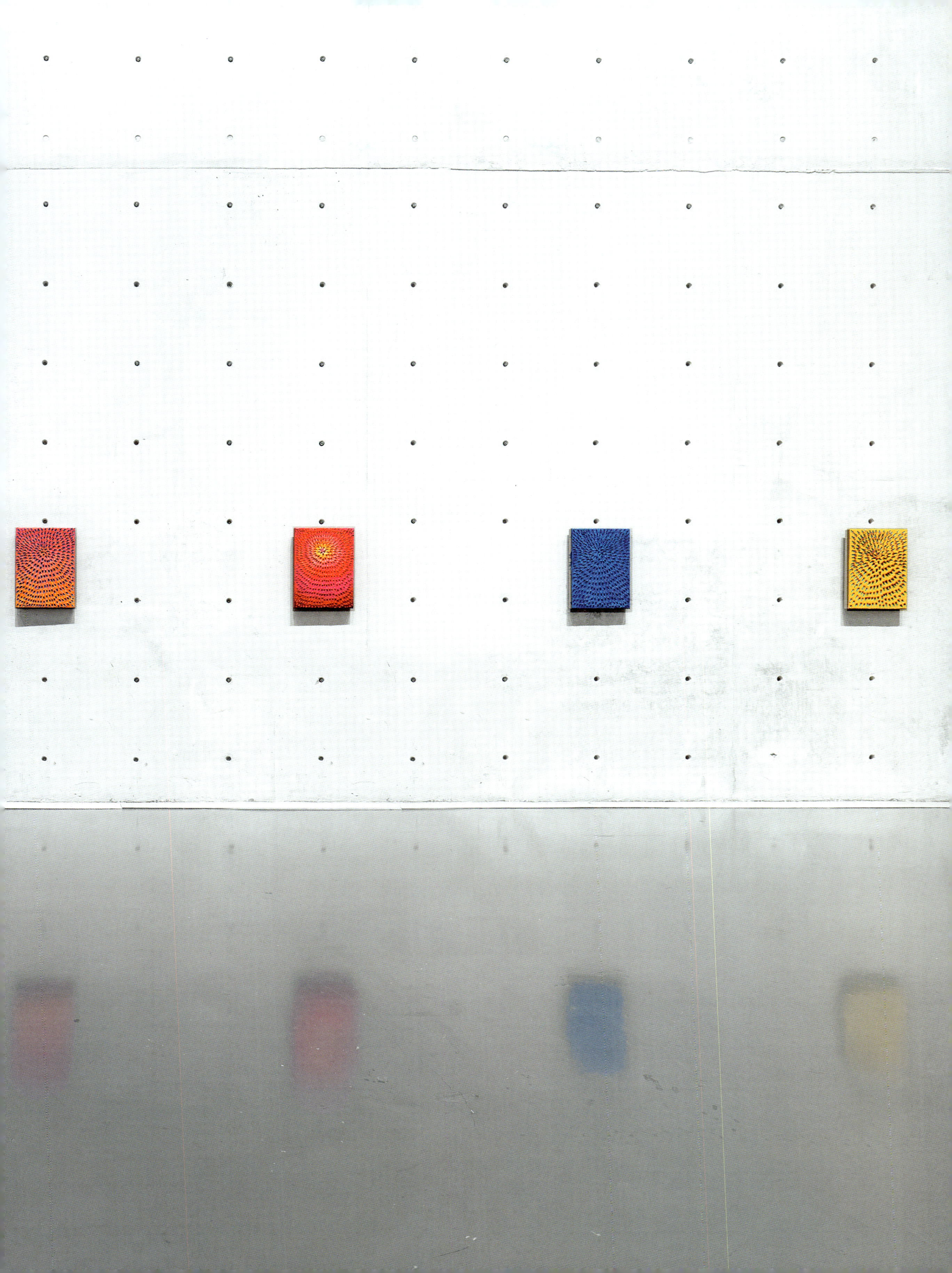

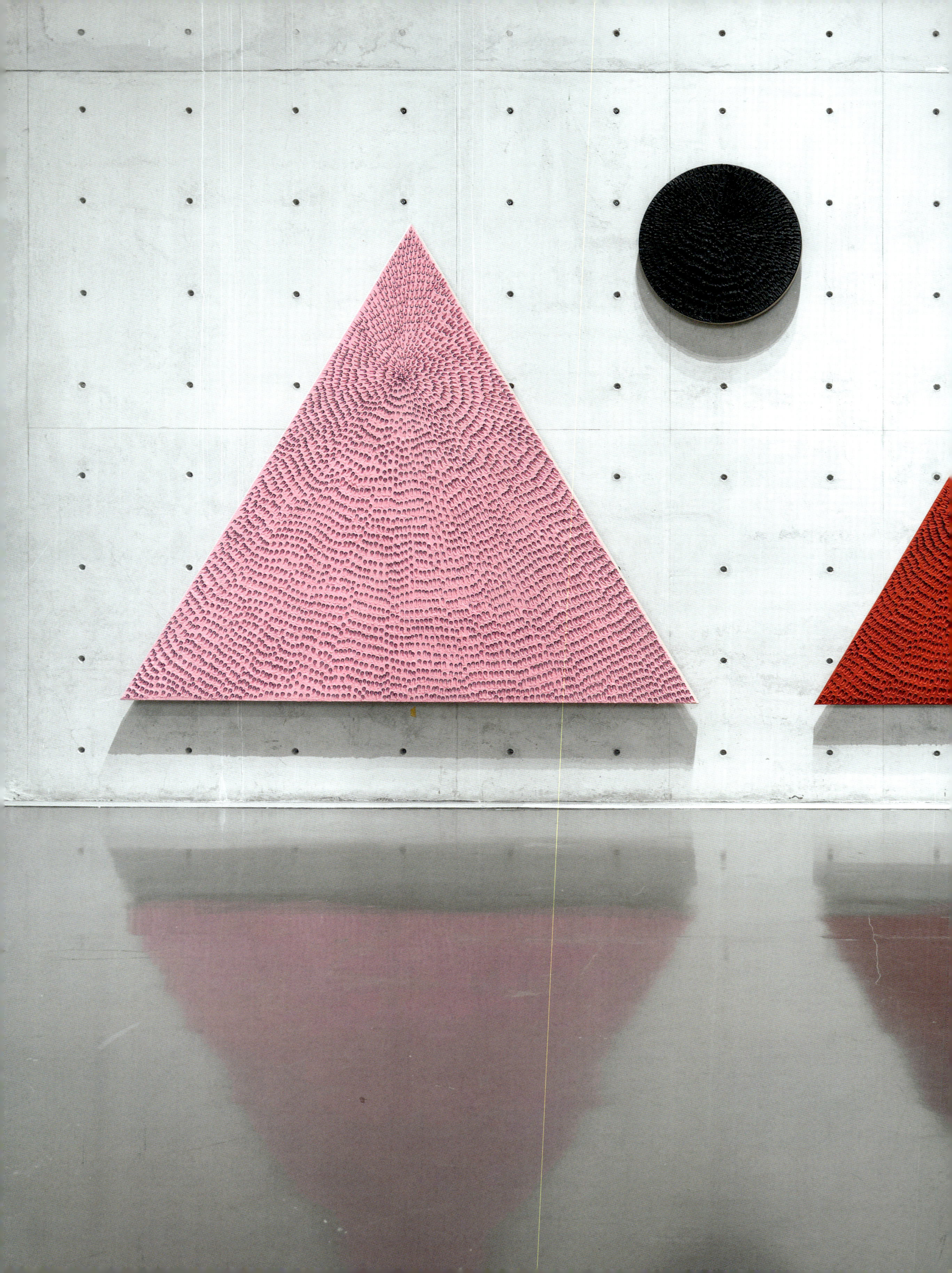

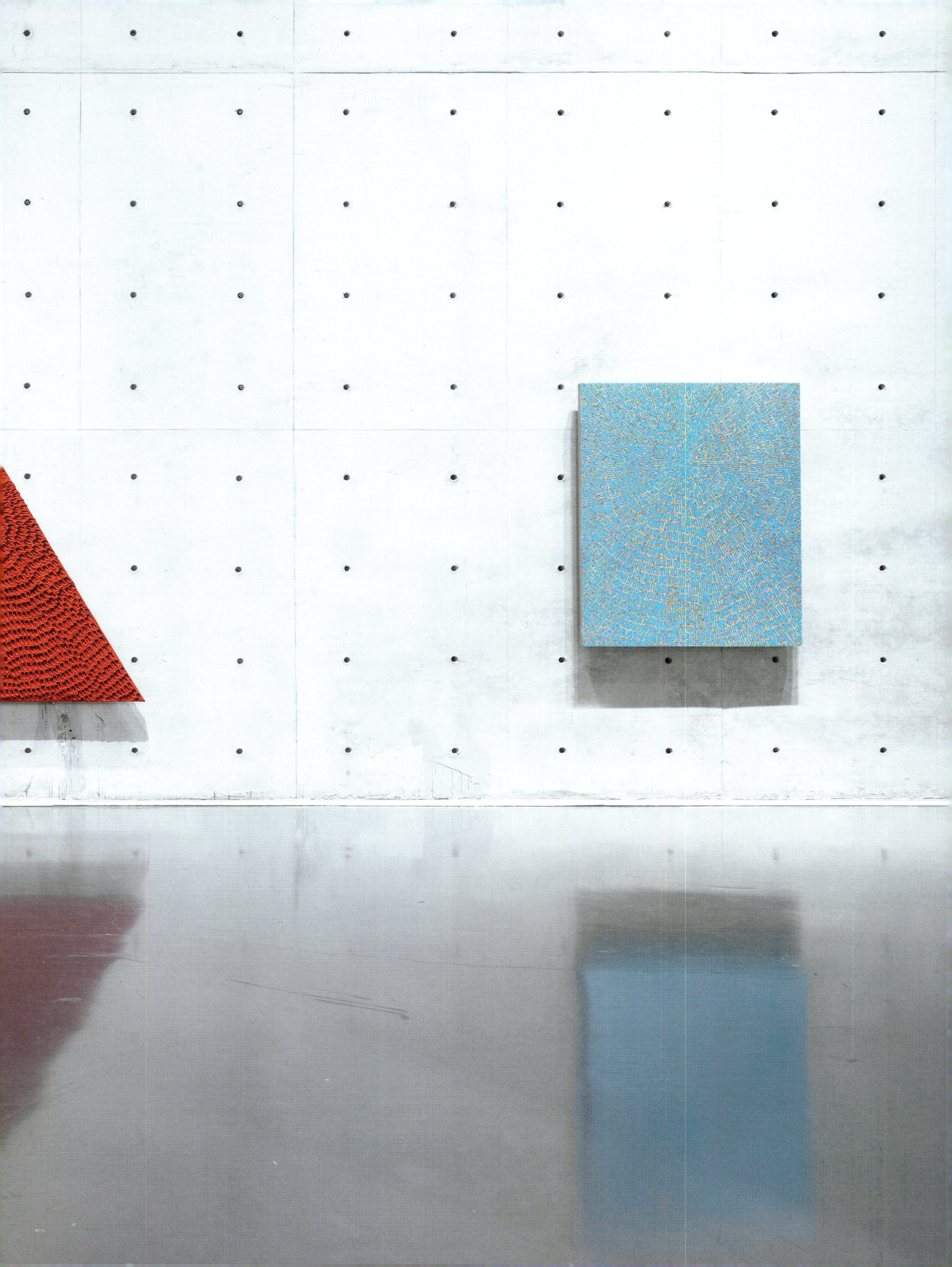

Works

Black Rainbow (Painted Black Sand SF #6F, Rainbow Ground, Black and Rainbow, Black CS), 2017
Sand, acrylic and oil on linen
92 x 74 inches

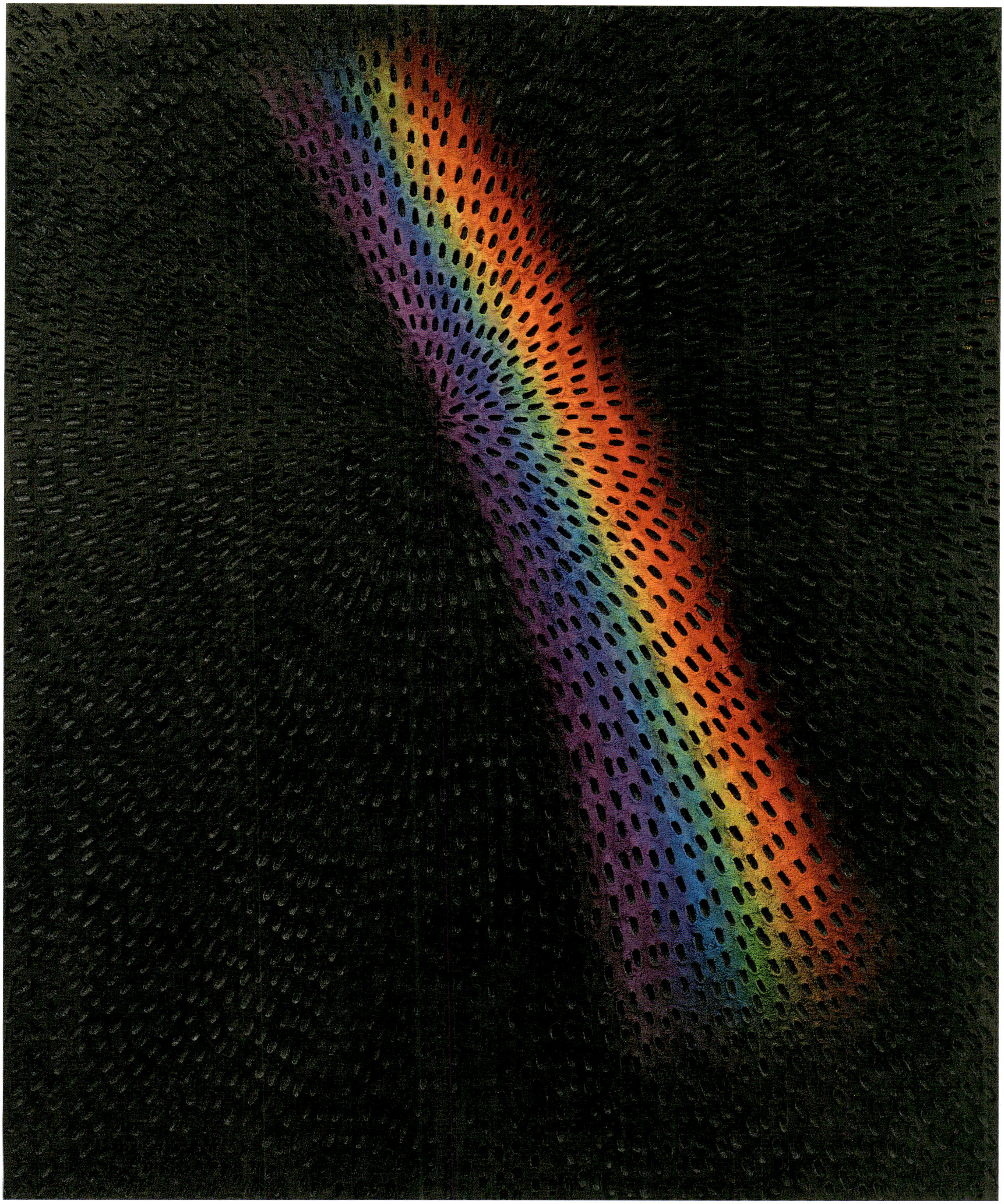

Rhythms of Nature (Painted Universe Mandala, Rainbow Gradient, Pink Ground), 2021–2022
Sand, acrylic and oil on linen
116 x 98 inches

Drawing inspiration from artists such as Jean Dubuffet, Wassily Kandinsky, Alberto Burri, Georges Braque, and Pablo Picasso—all of whom used sand at some point in their practice—Guidi is attracted by the physicality of the texture on canvas and the possibility of playing with contrast and depth on different surfaces. Echoing Goethe's color theory, the artist visually represents the belief in the profound effects of color and its impact on human behavior and explores the color spectrum, evoking metaphysical themes that transcend Western traditions. Guidi's diverse influences tie together spiritual references and scientific observation, providing a framework of concepts for her work, such as light refraction, geometry, and philosophy.

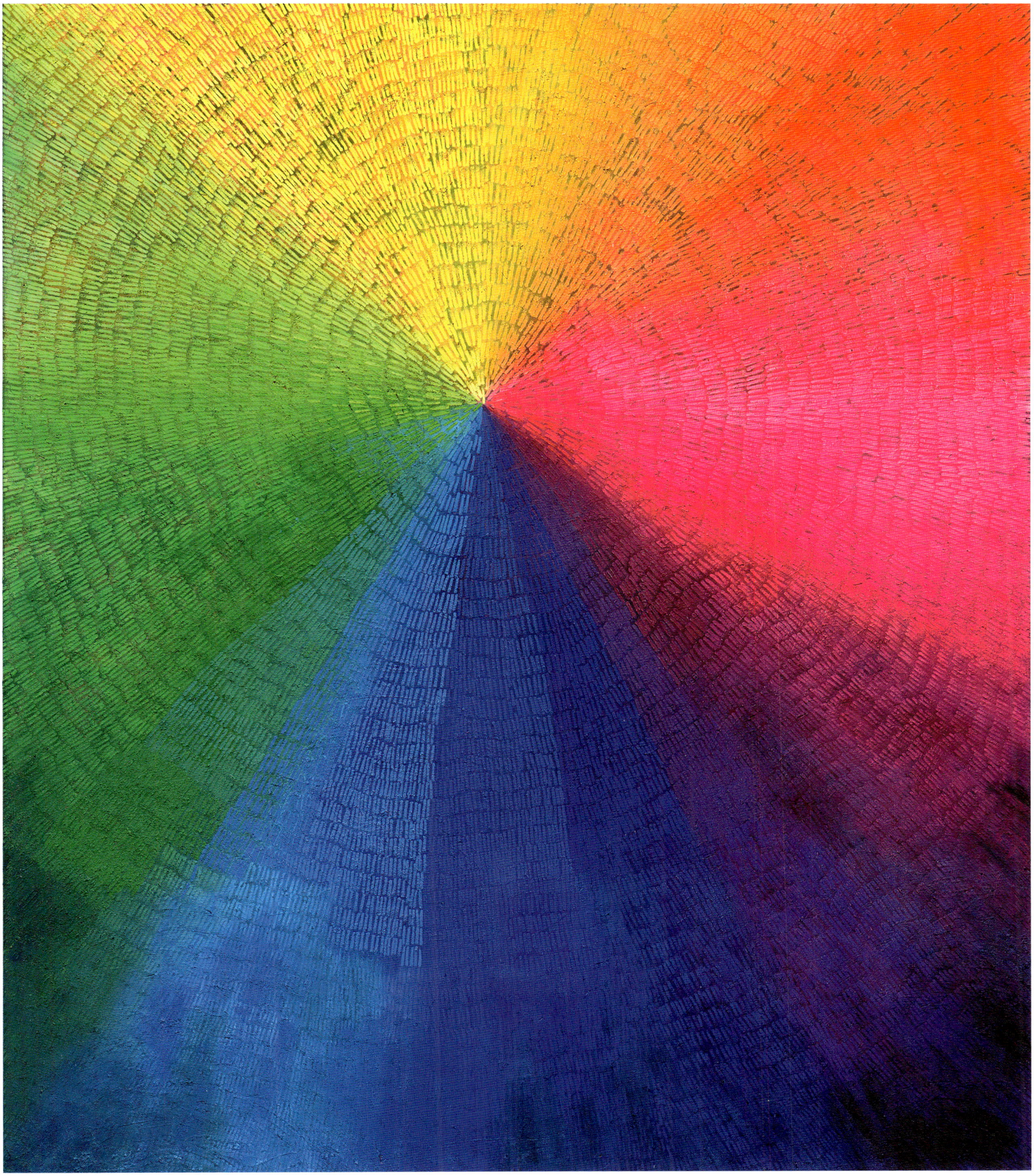

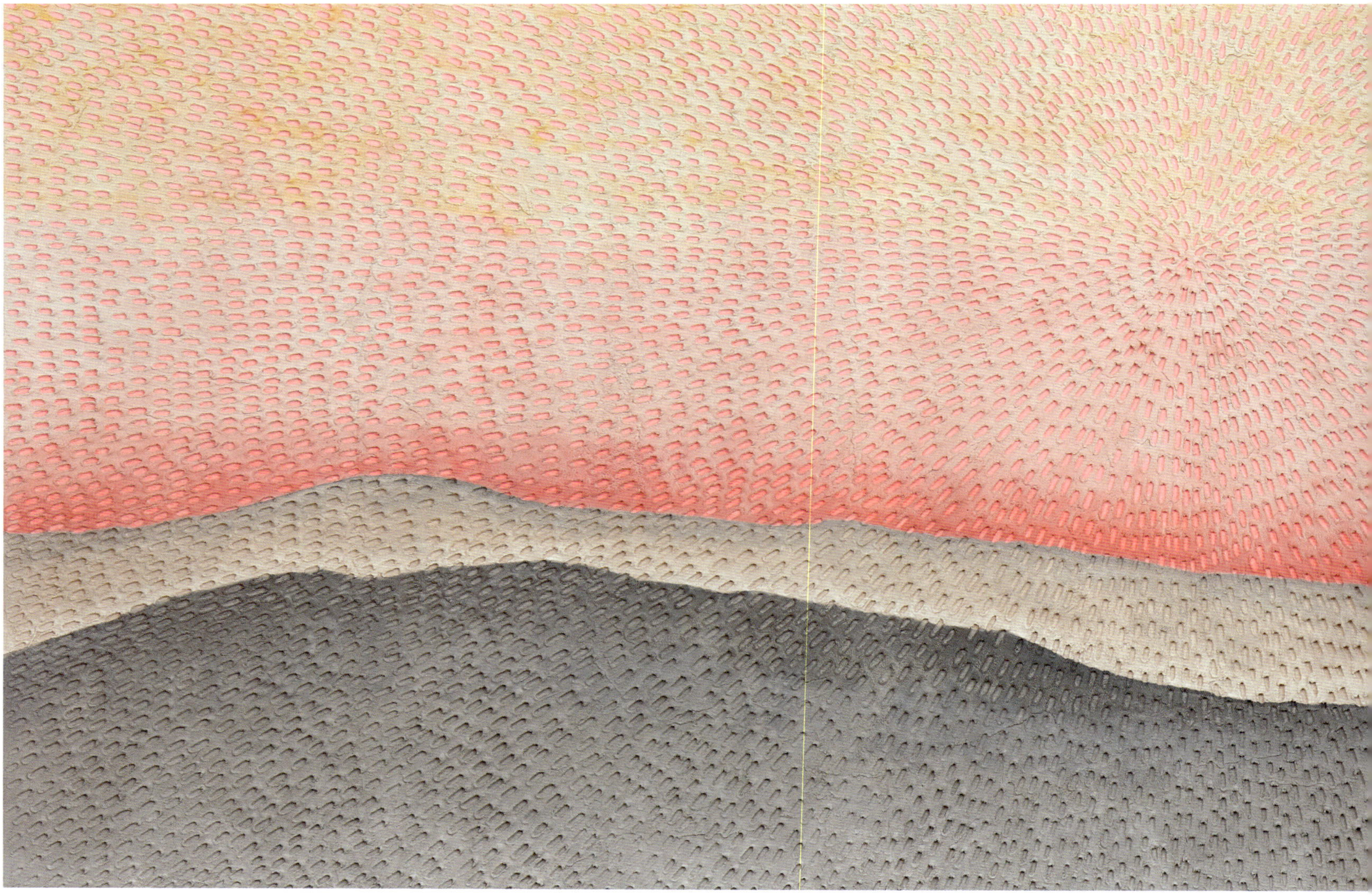

Thoughts Move Along Your Ridge
(Painted Sand SF #3P, Pink Sky), 2017
Sand, acrylic and oil on linen
76 x 232 inches

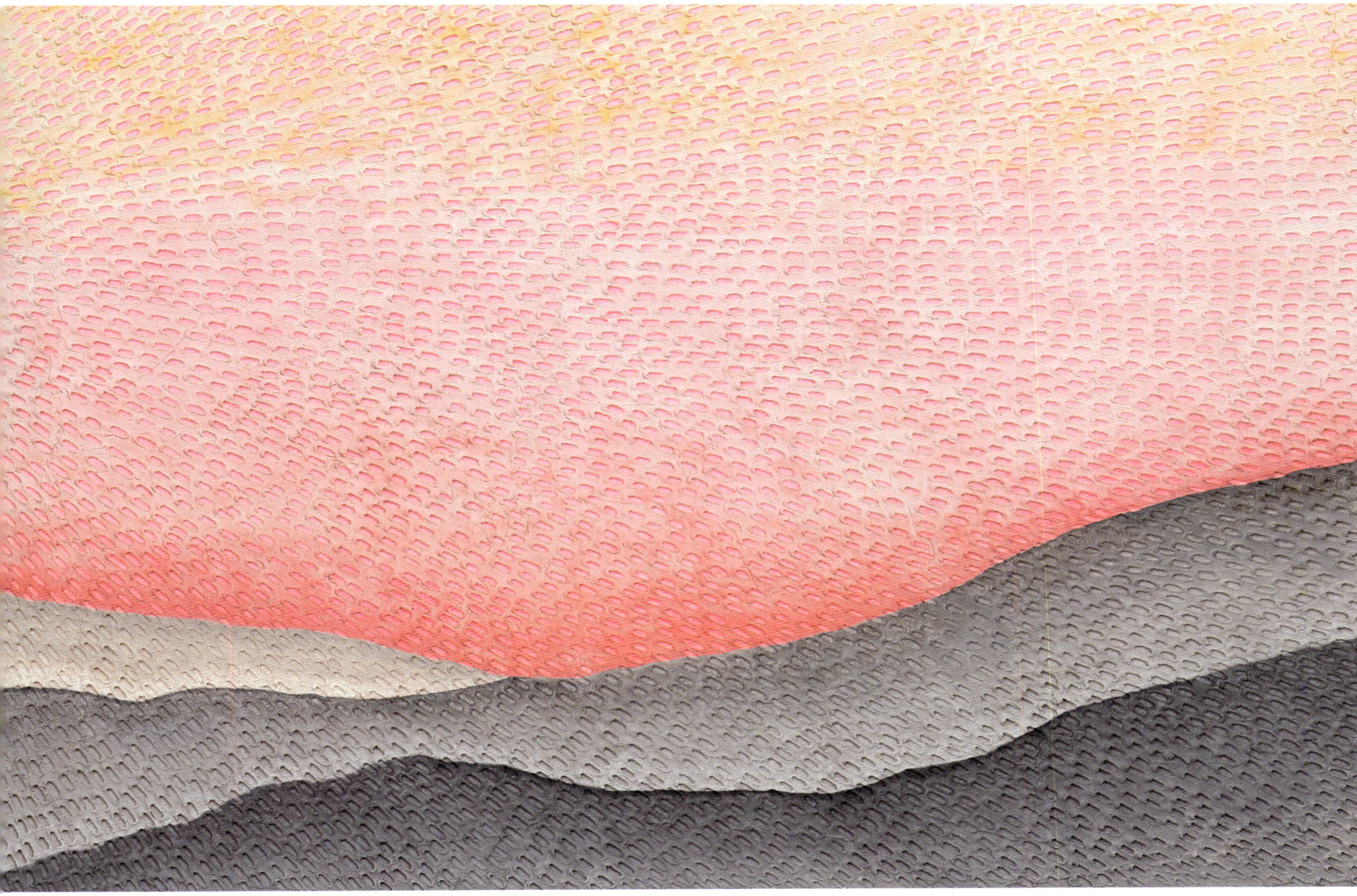

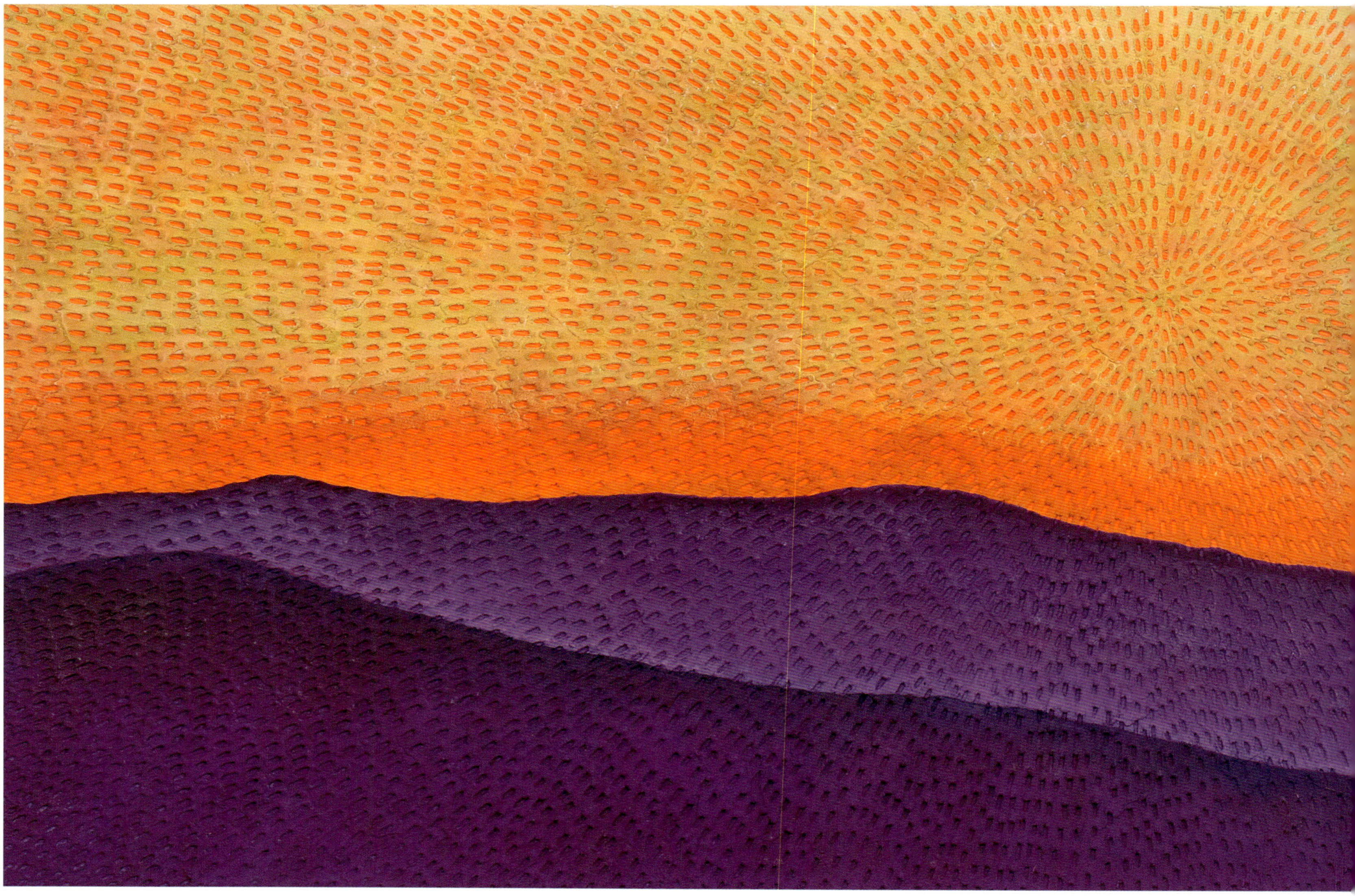

As I Drove You Stretched
(Painted Sand SF #1P, Orange Sky), 2017
Sand, acrylic and oil on linen
76 x 232 inches

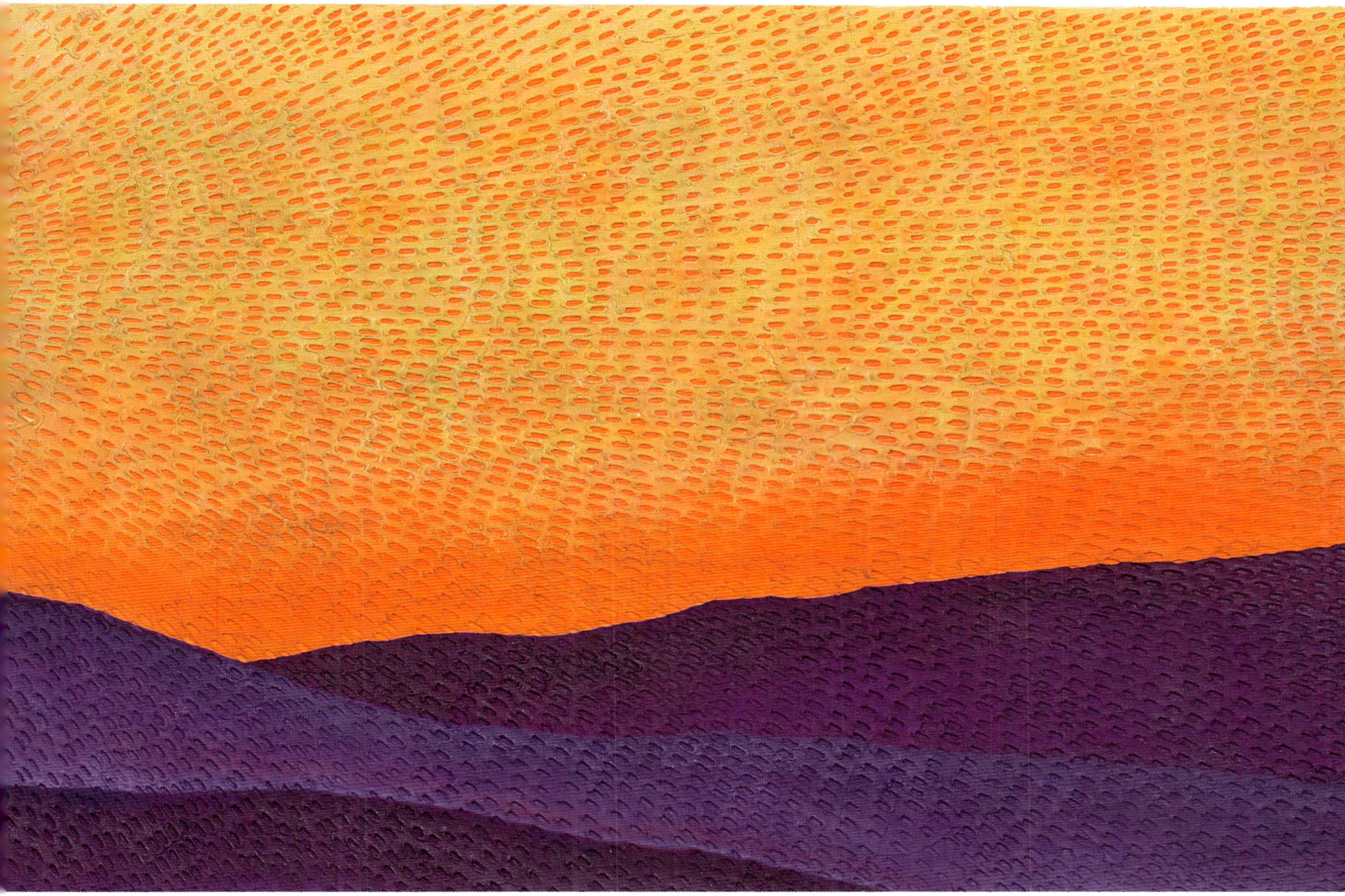

Majestic Mountains (Painted Yellow Sand SF #1H, Yellow-Pink-Light Orange-Dark Orange-Purple Sky, Black-Purple Mountain, Natural Ground), 2021
Sand, acrylic and oil on linen
60 x 48 inches

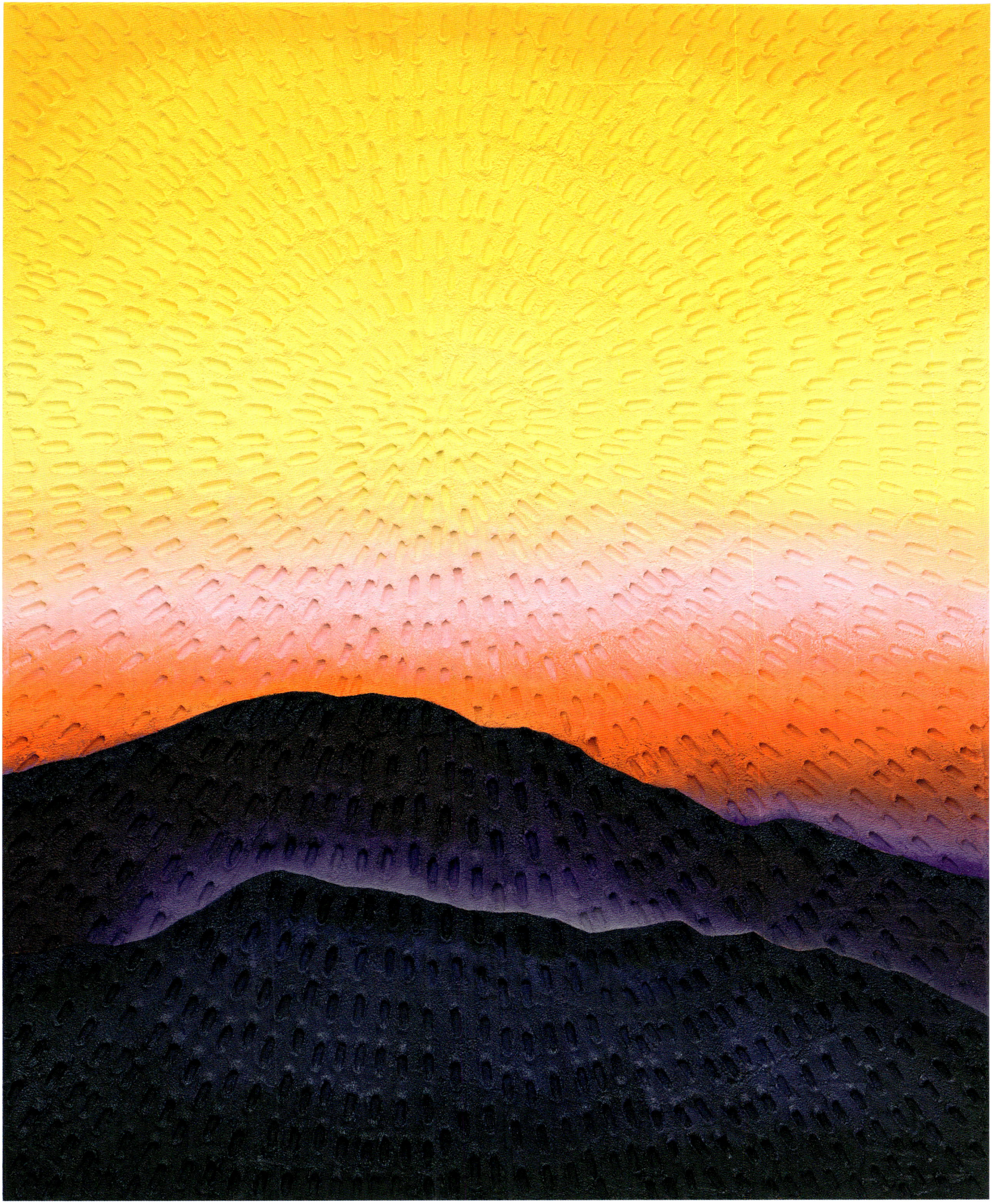

Soul Sings (Painted Lavender Sand, Yellow-Pink-Orange Sky, Gray-Purple-Blue-Green-Yellow-White-Orange Mountain), 2021
Sand, acrylic and oil on linen
21 x 15 inches

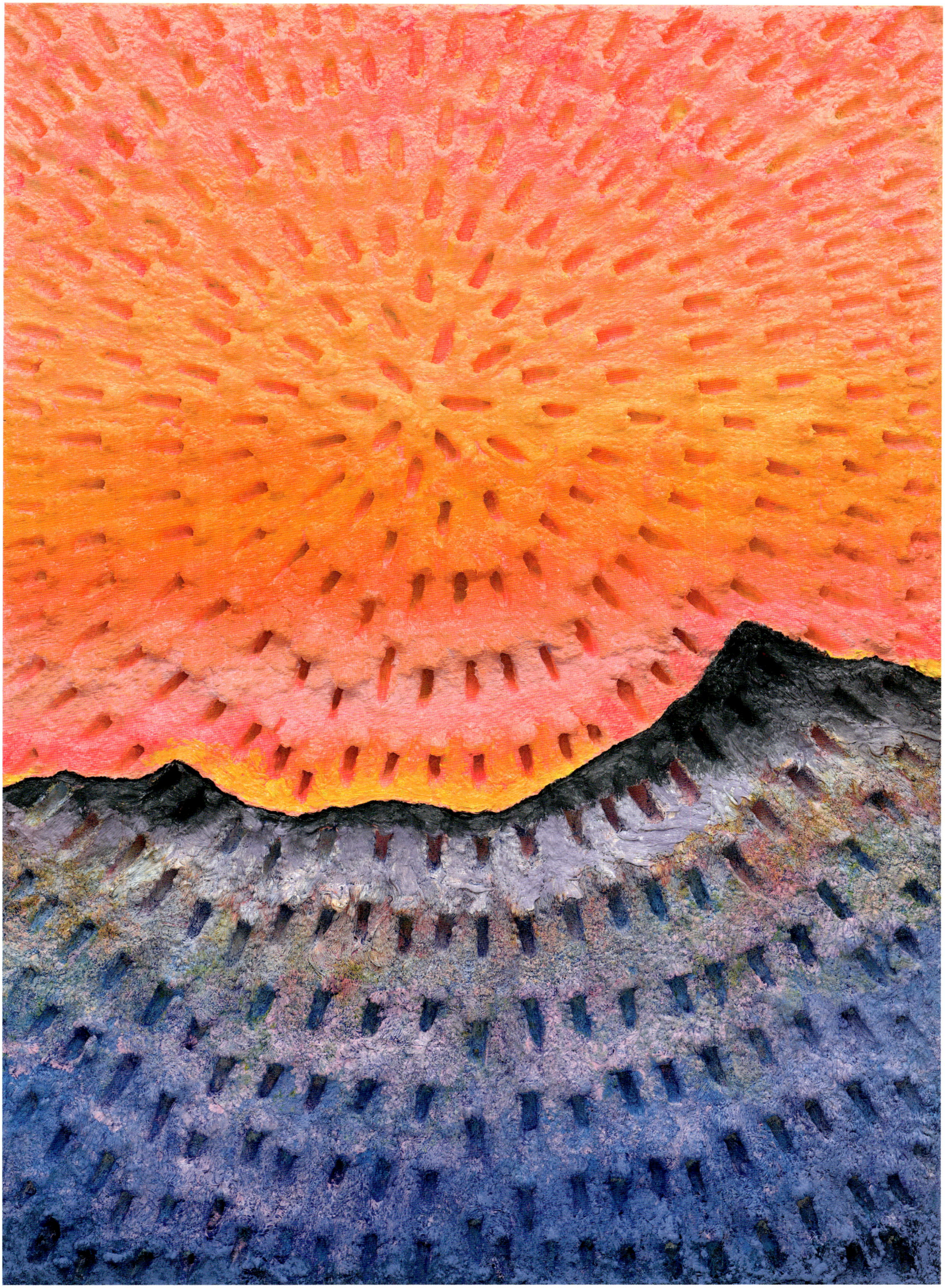

Follow Your Bliss (Painted White Sand, Yellow-Hot Pink Sky, Purple Gradient Mountain, Blue Highlight), 2021
Sand, acrylic and oil on linen
21 x 15 inches

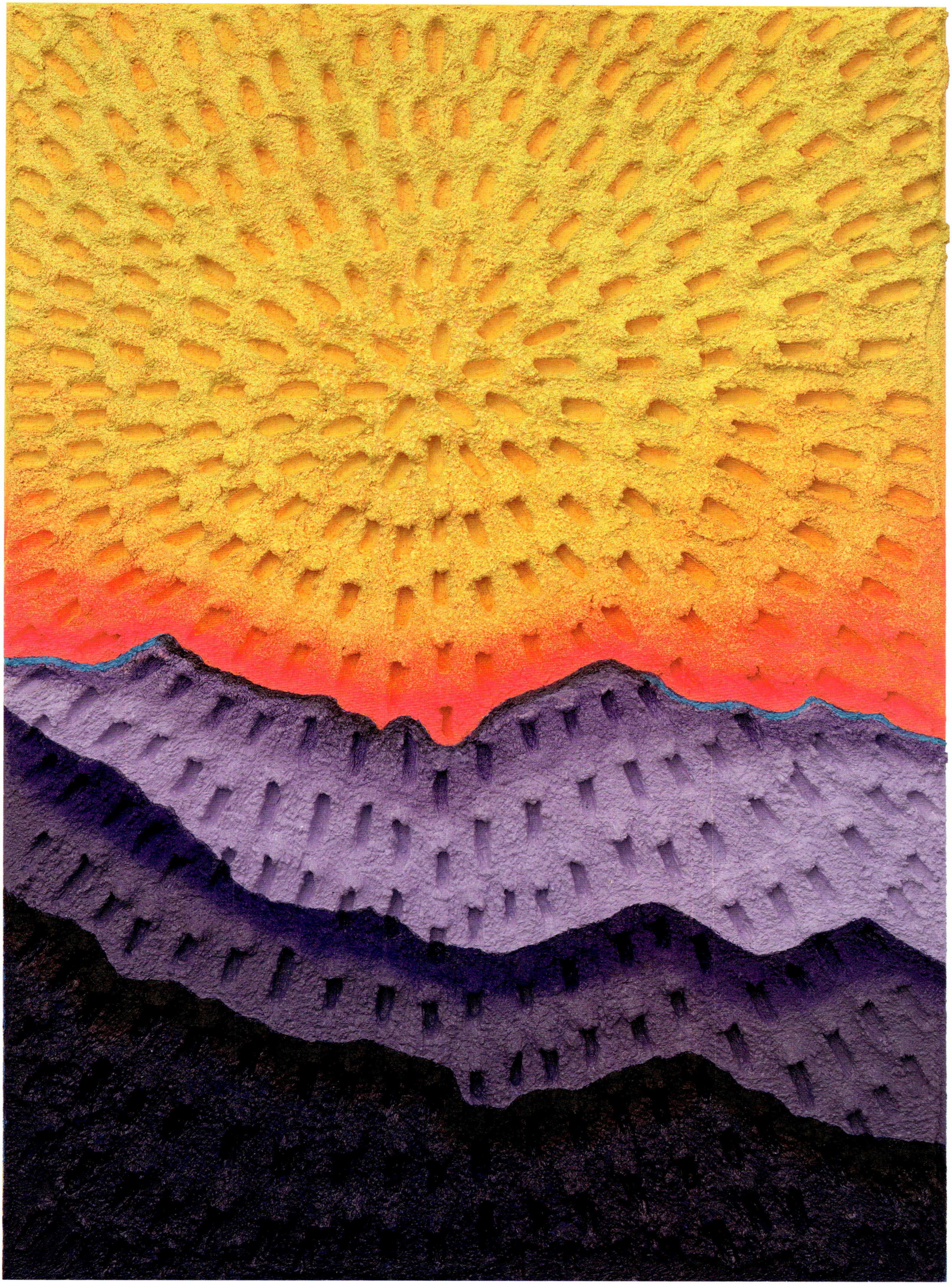

Moonlight and Love (Painted Pink Sand, Black-Dark Blue-Purple-Pink-Green-Yellow Sky, Yellow-Purple-Dark Purple-Pink-Red Mountain), 2021
Sand, acrylic and oil on linen
21 x 15 inches

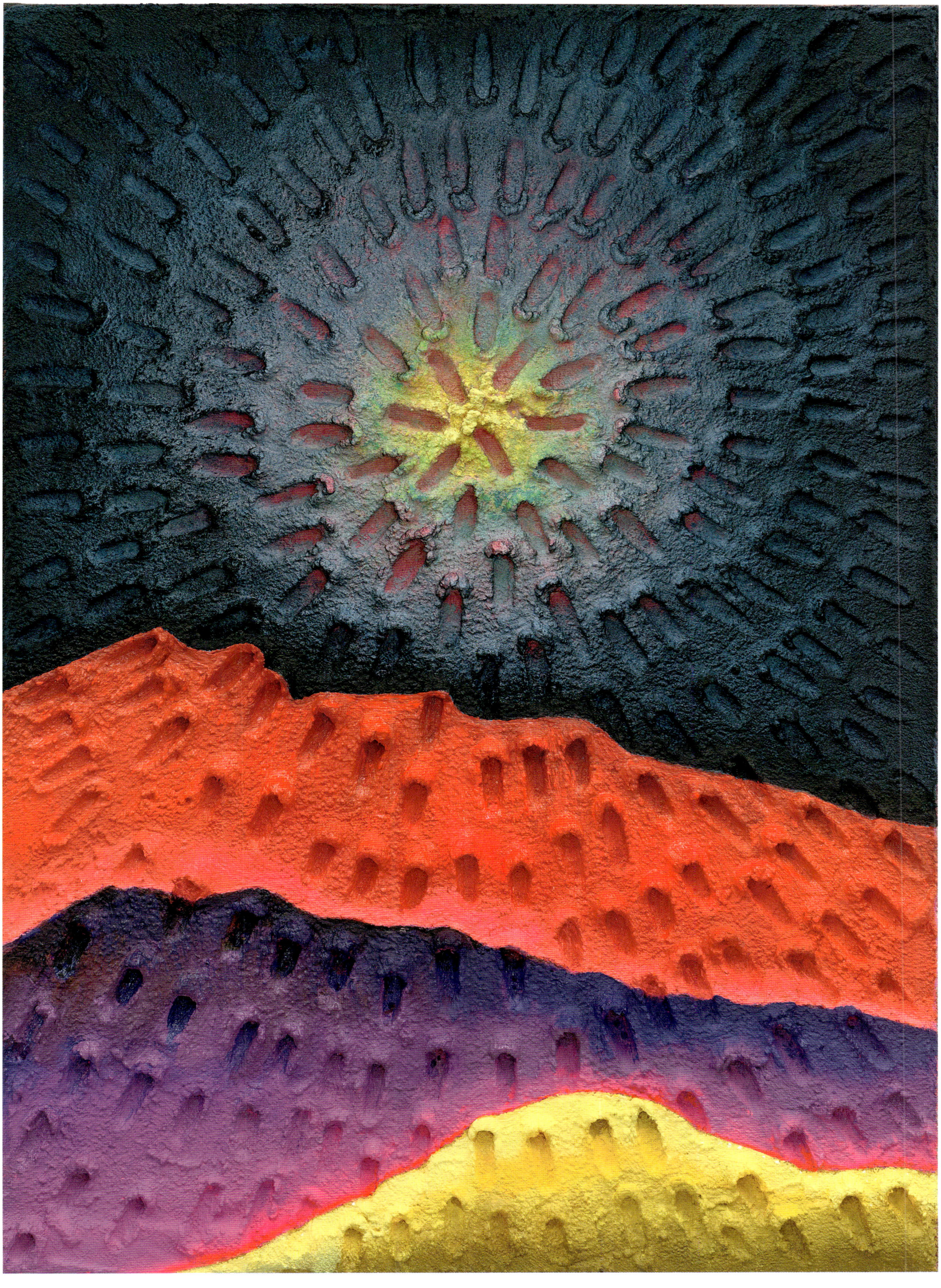

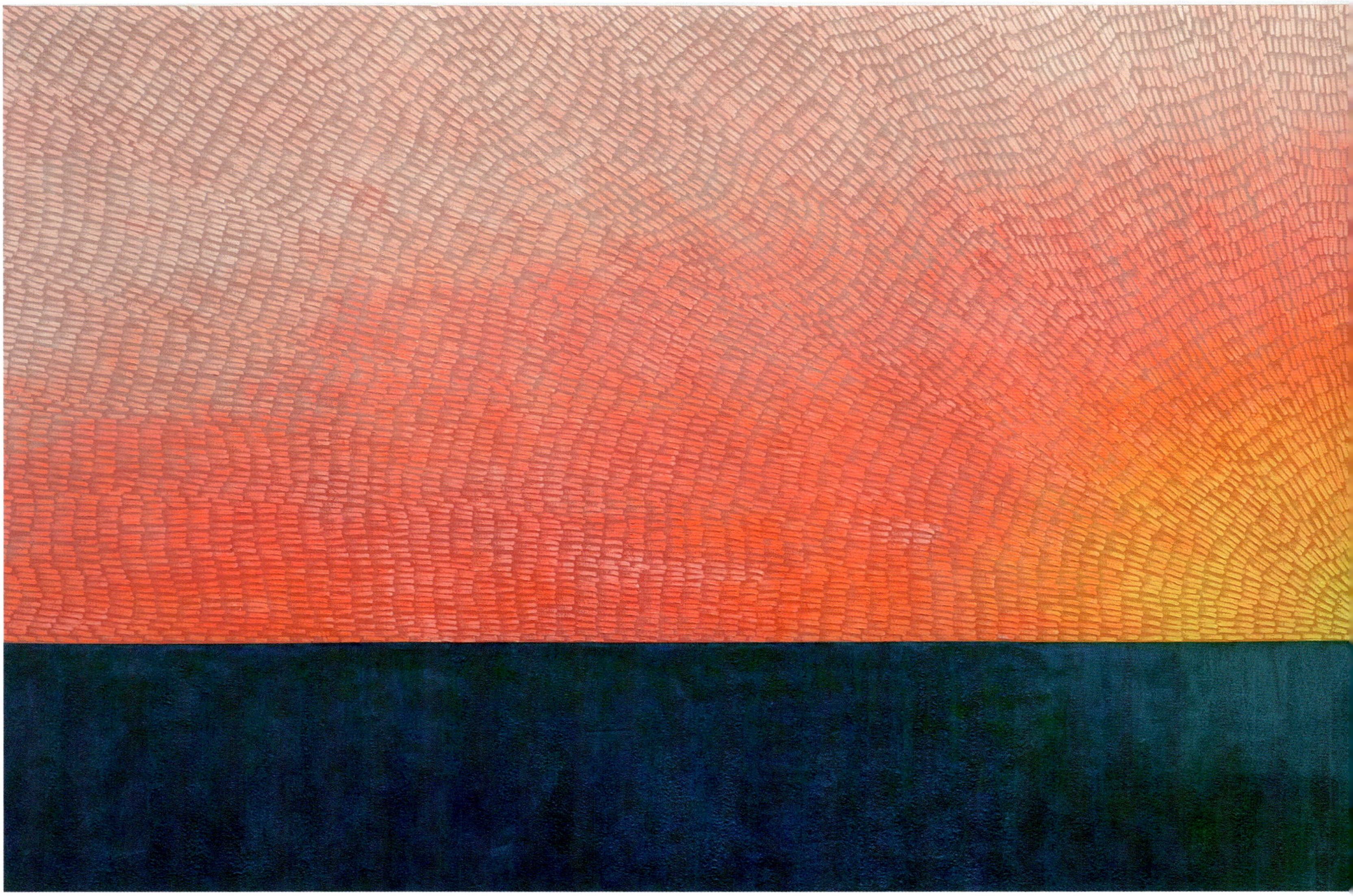

A New Beginning, 2019–2020
Sand, acrylic and oil on linen
76 x 232 inches

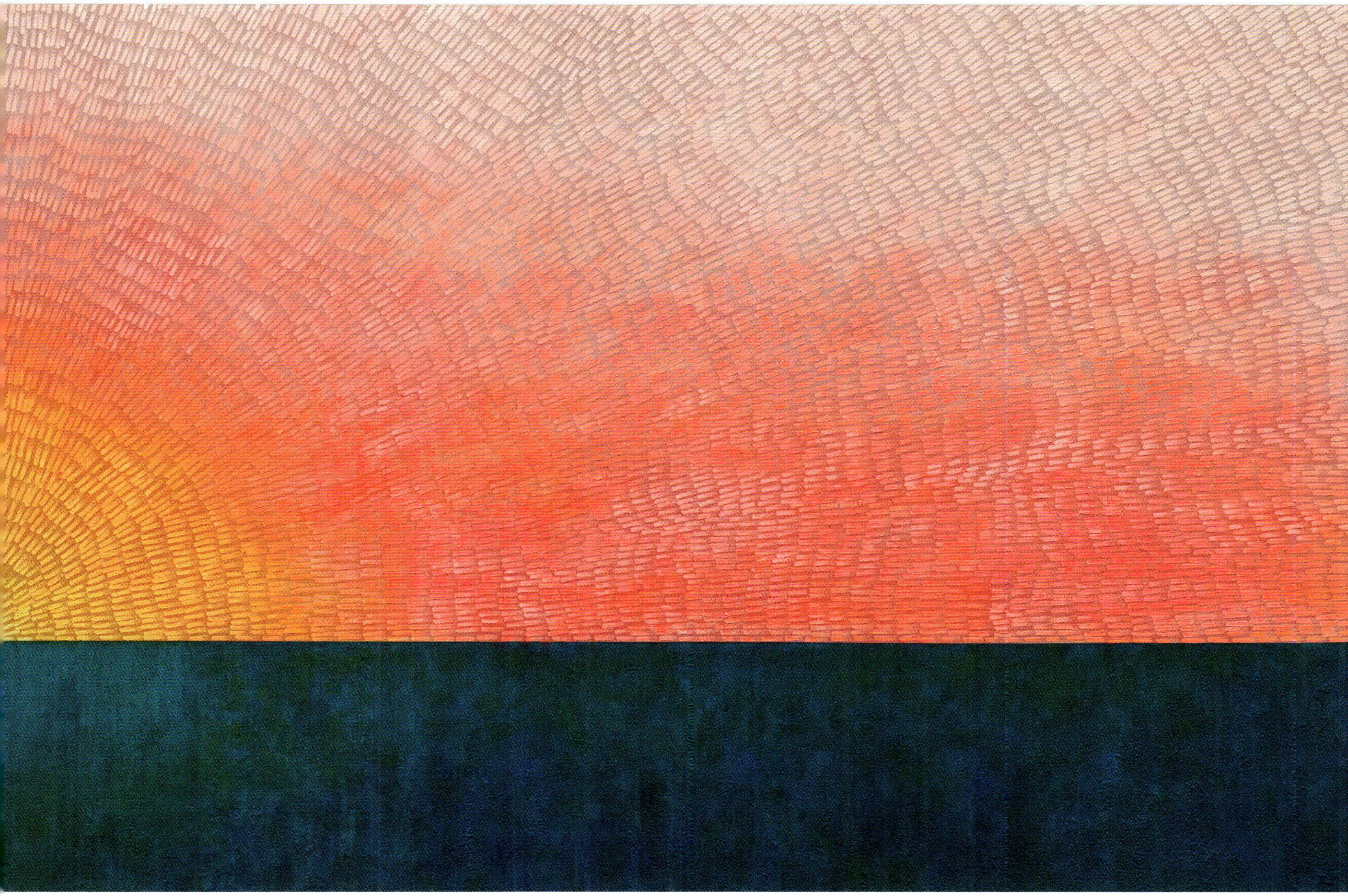

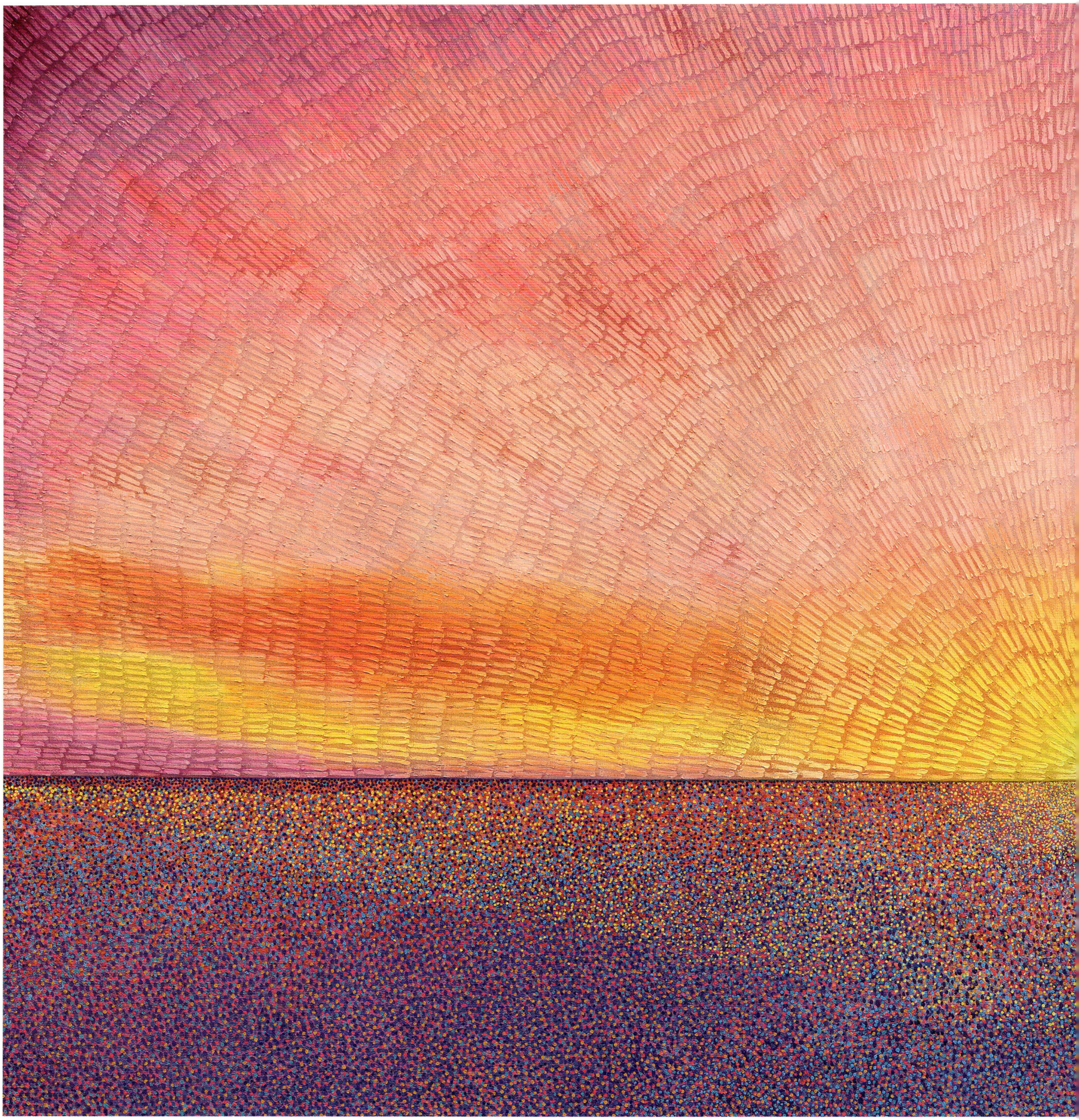

Beyond the Sea (Painted Sand Horizon, Purple-Pink-Orange-Yellow Sunrise Gradient), 2021–2022
Sand, acrylic and oil on linen
76 x 144 inches

Beyond the Sea is an immersive sunset sand painting marked by tonal and chromatic shifts combined with a richly granular surface. The heliocentric composition exemplifies Guidi's inquisitive practice rooted in the repetition of signs.
The formal result goes beyond the boundaries of objective reality to enter a meditative and hypnotizing landscape. The artist creates an intuitive language through energy and sensory stimulation based on her investigation of color and mark-making.

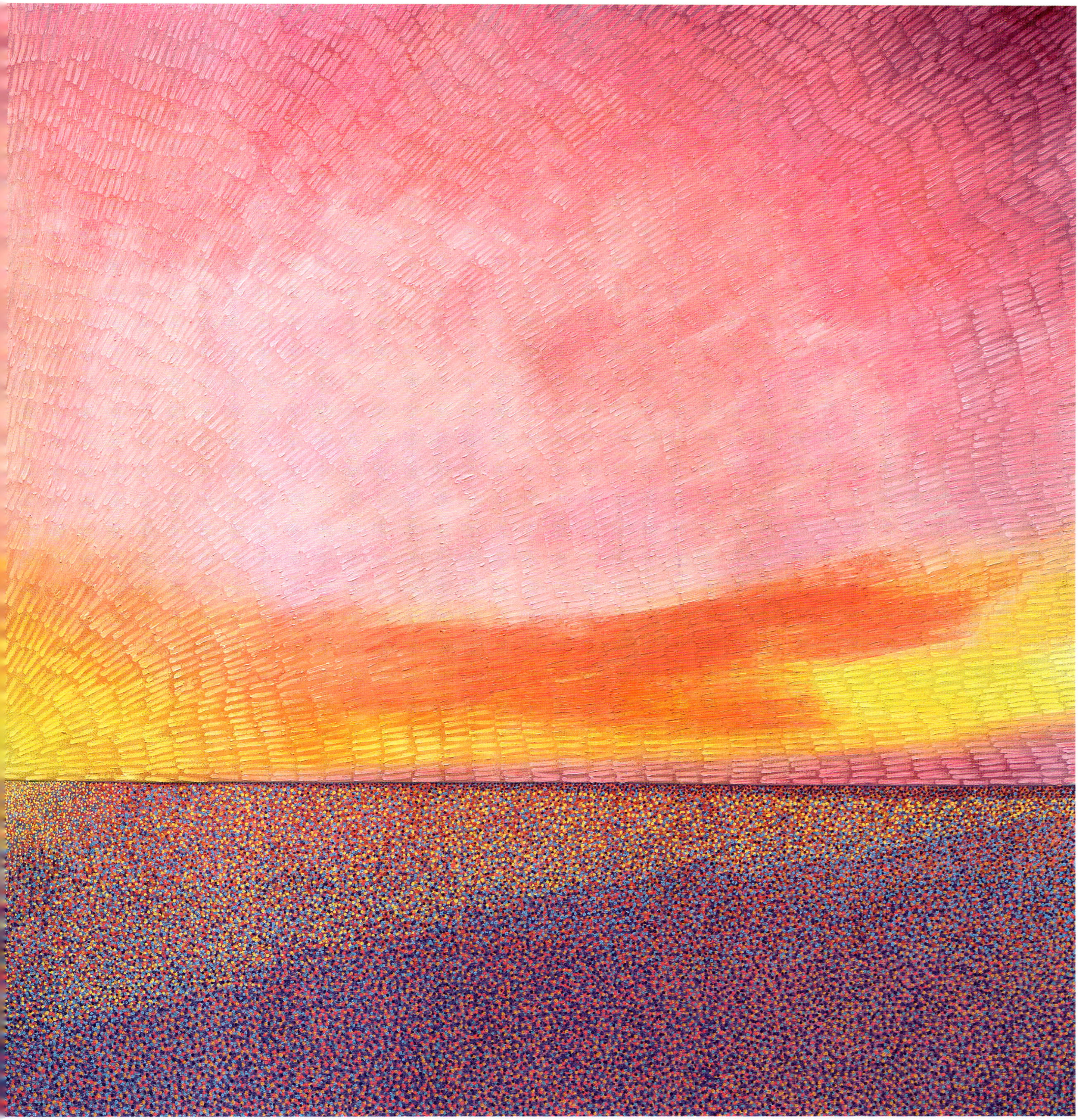

Between the Earth and Sun (Black Sand, Black Ground; Black MT, Pink Sand, Pink CS, Pink Ground; Black MT, Red Sand, Red CS, Red Ground), 2021–2022
Sand, acrylic and oil on linen
Circle: 36 inch diameter
Large triangle: 108 x 126 inches
Small triangle: 66 x 76 inches

The triptych is a recurrent composition in Guidi's formal vocabulary, here developed in a minimalistic representation of two mountains and/or pyramids and a new moon, balancing earthly and celestial forces. The new moon symbolizes new beginnings, and it is a time to set intentions for the month ahead. Guidi's incorporation of sand into her works represents the result of the tireless weathering of rocks over millions of years; a scientific process, but also a metaphor for the passing of time.

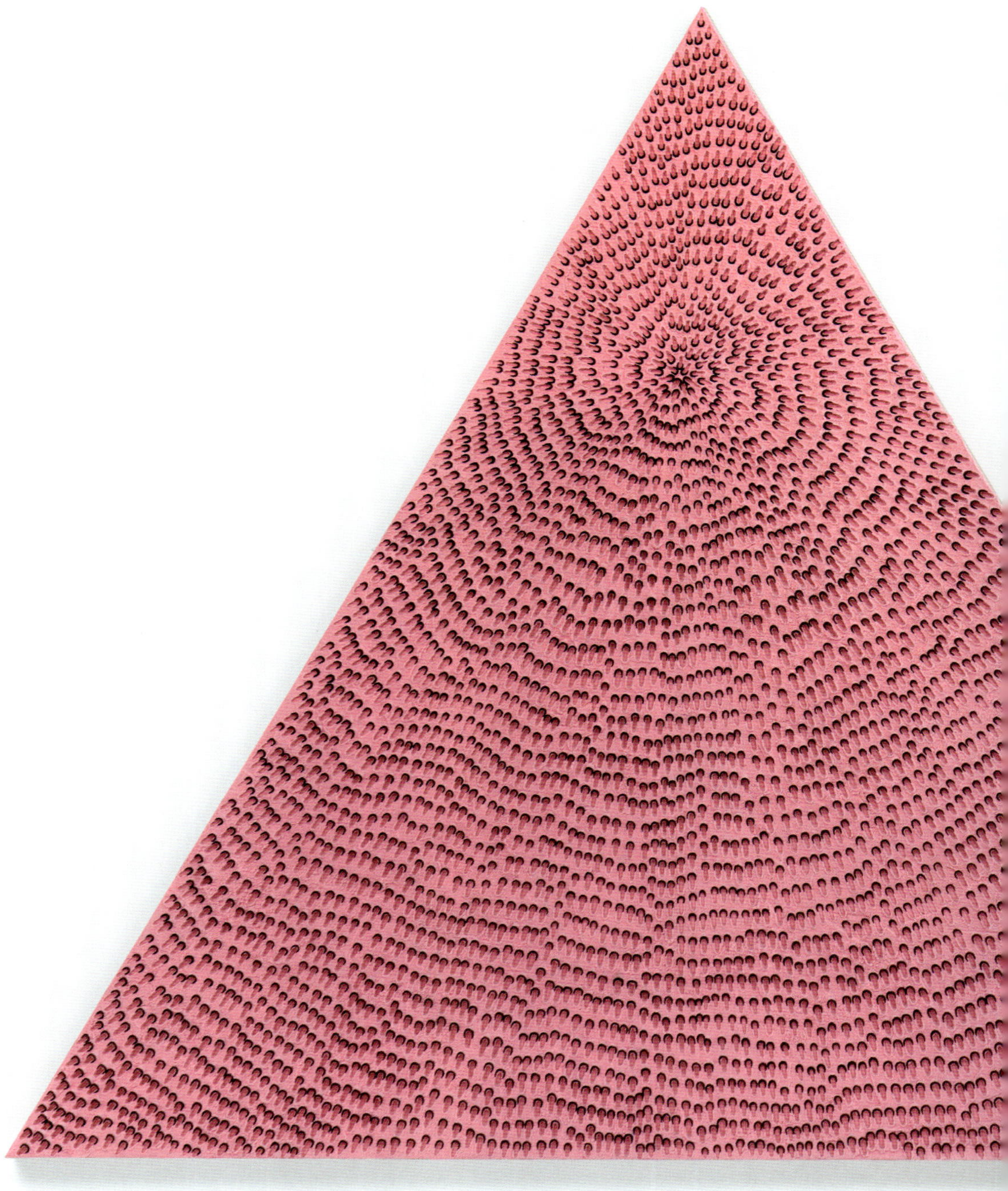

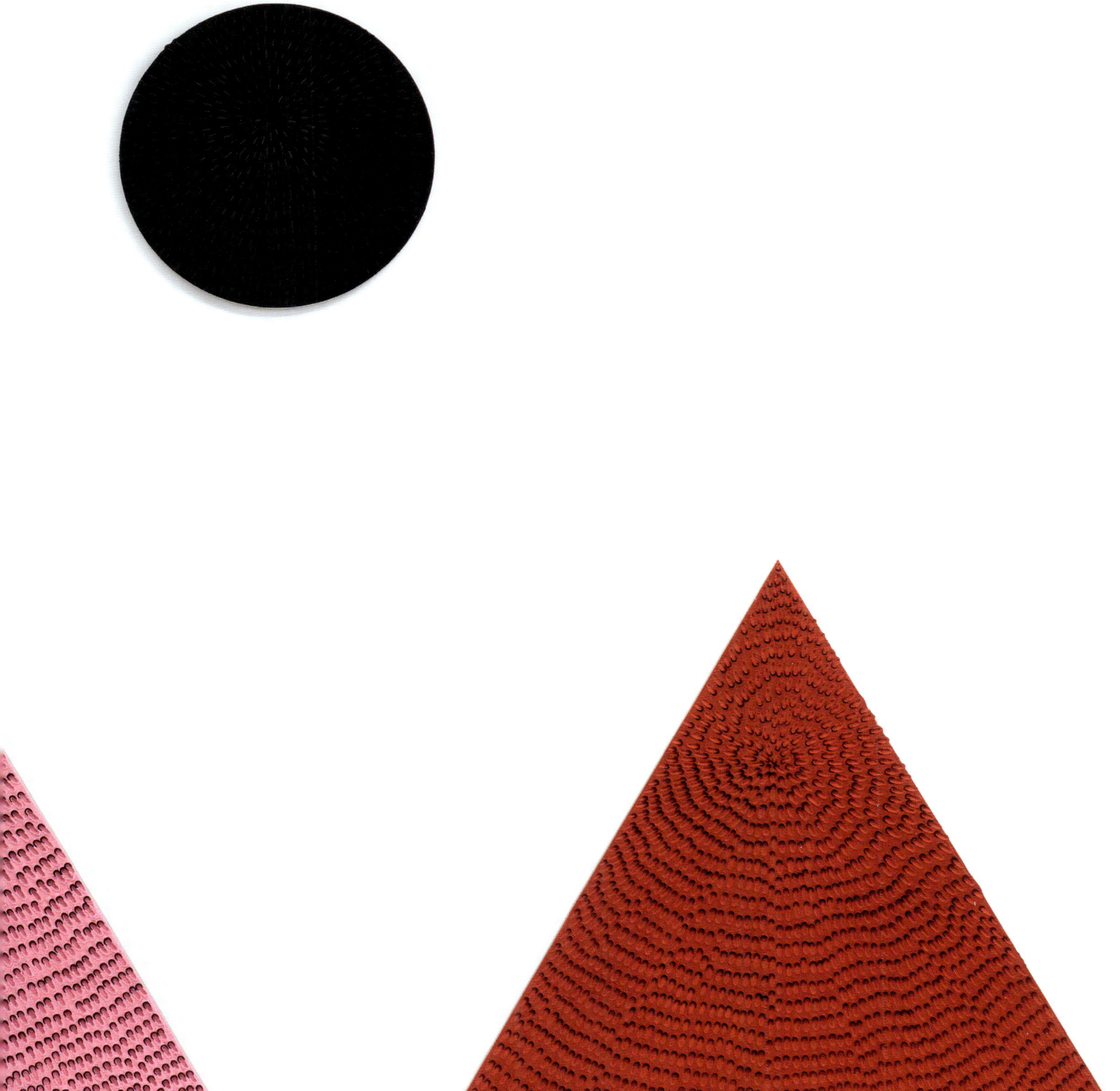

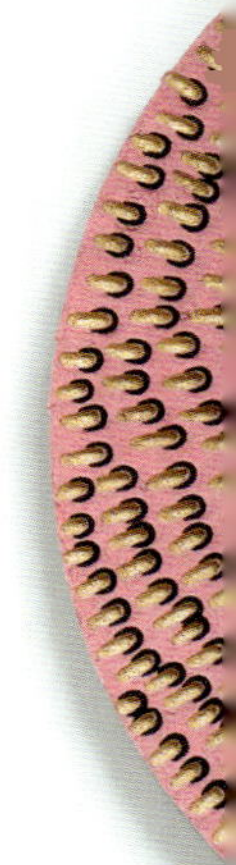

Born Under the Pink Moon
(Black MT, Pink Sand, Pink CS, Gold, Pink Ground; Gold PT, Black Sand, Black Ground),
2021–2022
Sand, acrylic and oil on linen
Circle: 36 inch diameter
Each snake: 66 x 49 inches

Subverting traditional Western triptych composition, Guidi forges a connection between Minimalism and mysticism. The twinned rising snakes suggest the archetypal symbol of rebirth and transformation, sinuously alluding to the infinity sign. The inclusion of a pink moon anticipates the arrival of springtime, a reassuring and confirmatory sign of the cycle of the seasons. Guidi is always looking for balance and symmetry as synonyms of peacefulness and calm.

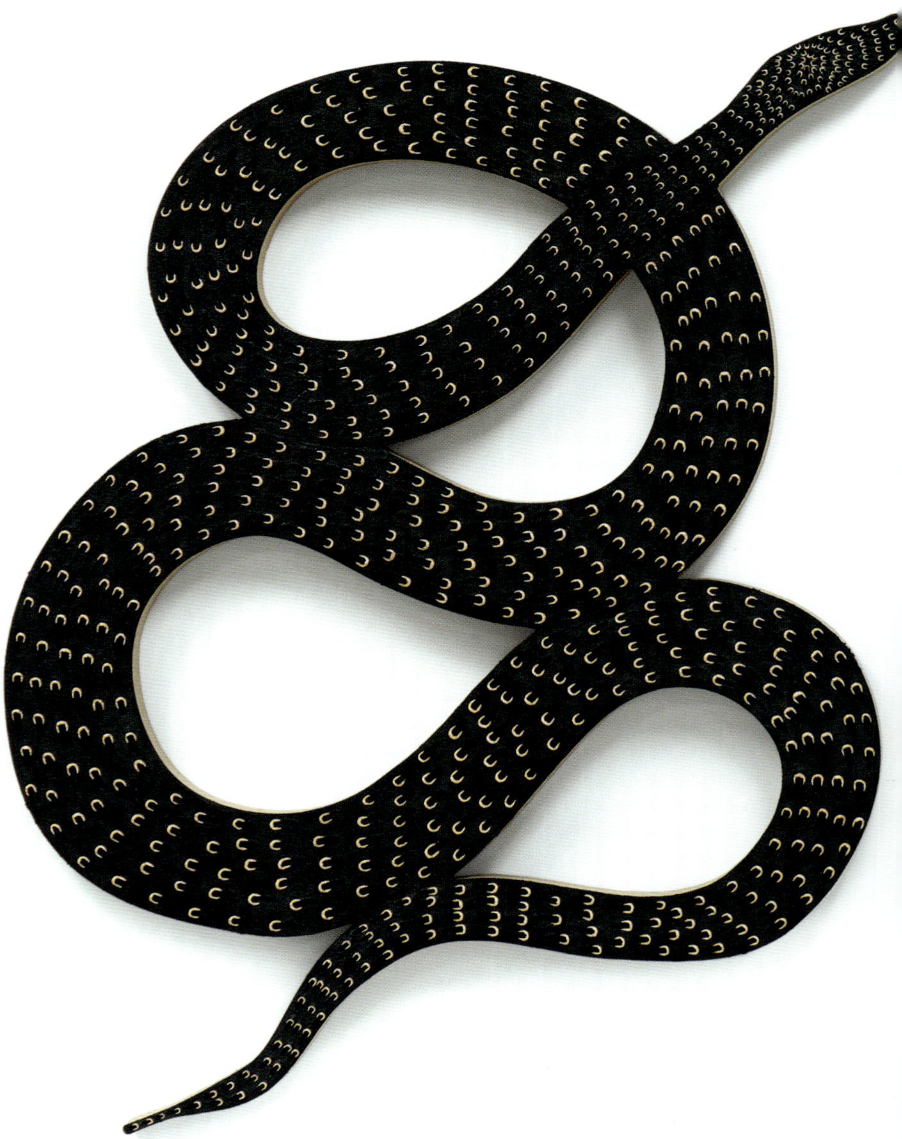

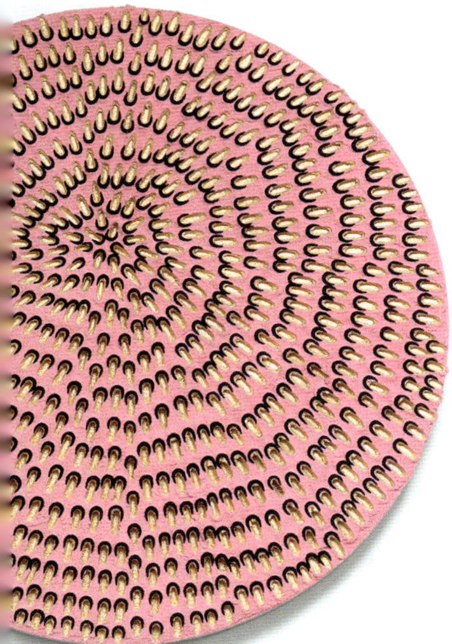

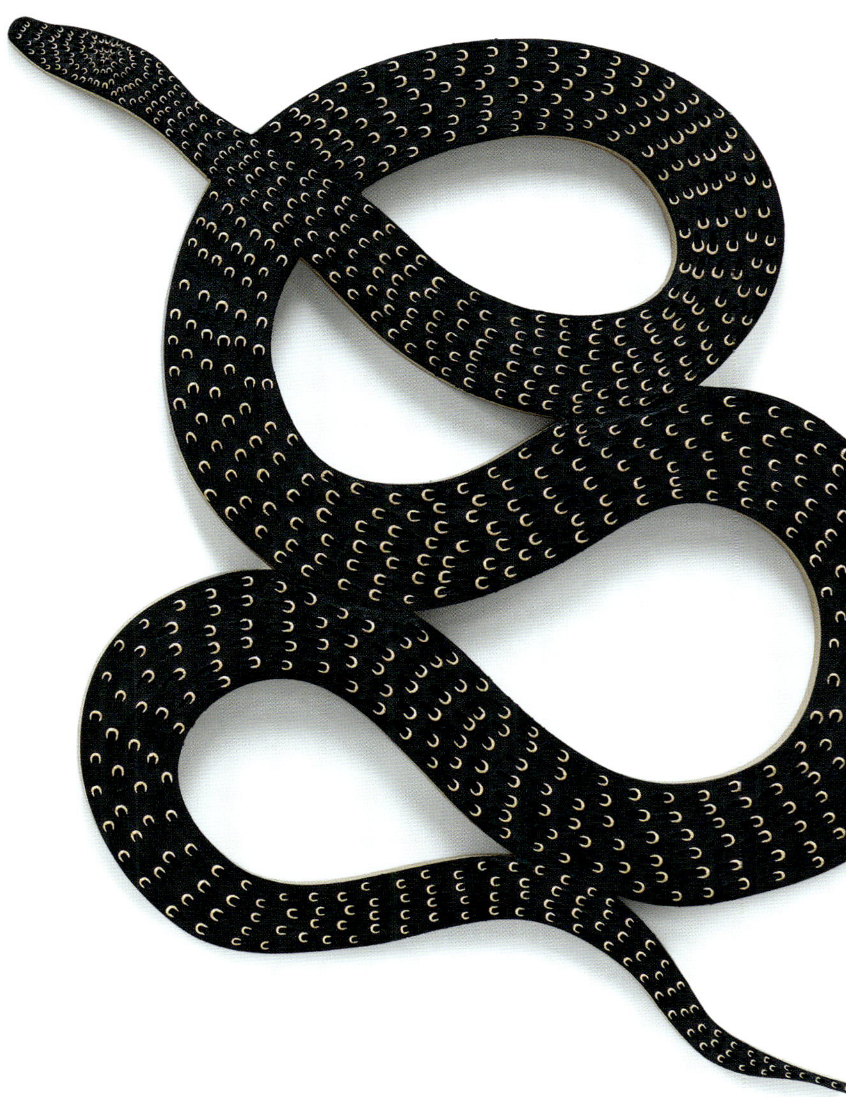

Lotus Wheel Manipura (Seven Chakras), 2022
Sand, acrylic and oil on linen
24 inch diameter

Lotus Wheel (Seven Chakras), 2021–2022 is composed of seven circular paintings that synthesize the idea of chakras as vital focal points of energy along the spine. The word "chakra" in Sanskrit translates to "wheel" or "circle," alluding to perpetual transformation. The process of these paintings begins with oil-wash underpaintings of chakra symbols that correspond to each surface color. In between is a layer of meticulously placed dots of oil paint in varying colors. These seven paintings further Guidi's recent exploration of incorporating Impressionist influences into her artwork. This fusion of East meets West is a familiar theme for Guidi.

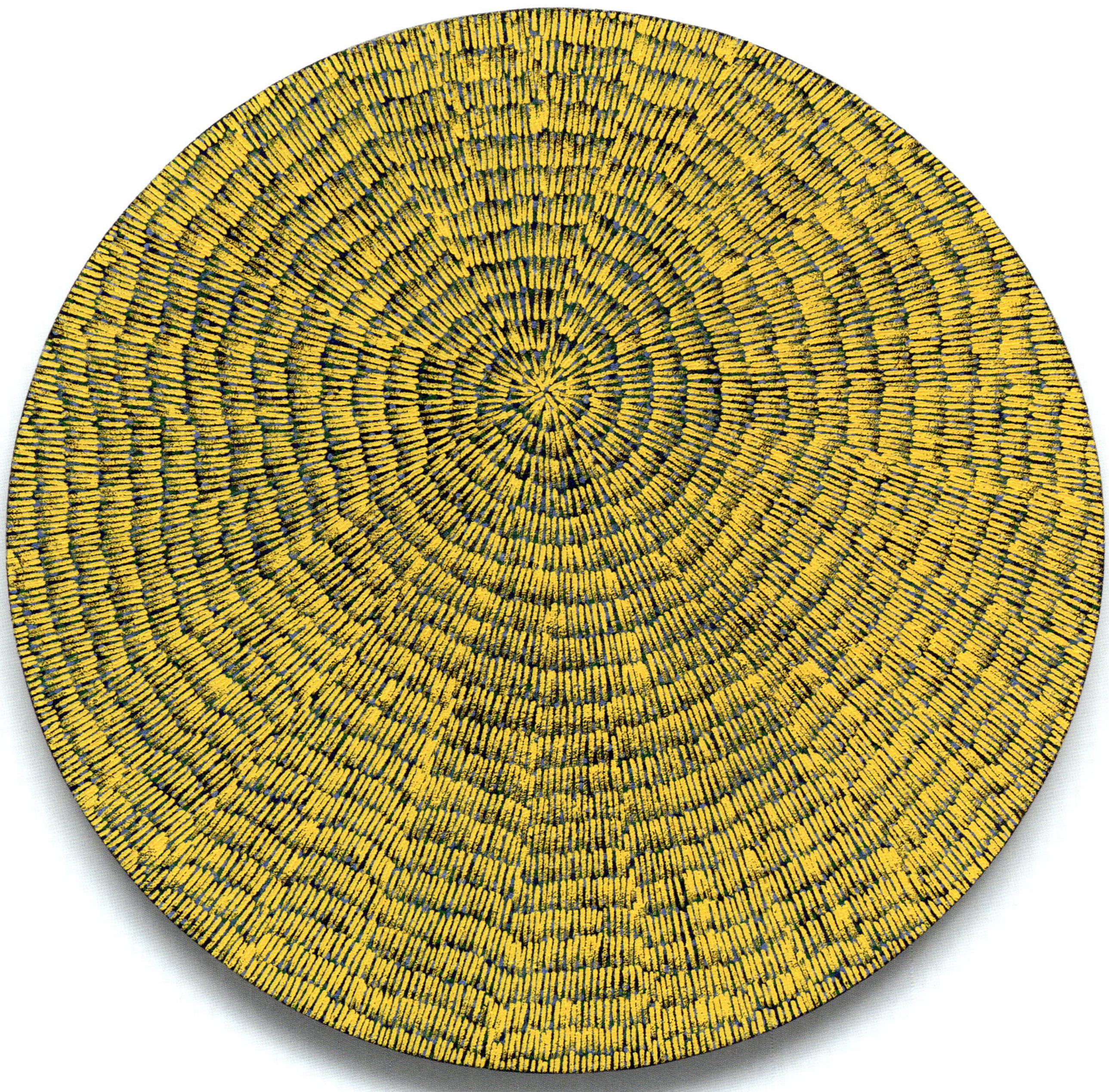

Lotus Wheel Sahasrara (Seven Chakras), 2021
Sand, acrylic and oil on linen
24 inch diameter

Lotus Wheel Anahata
(Seven Chakras), 2022
Sand, acrylic and oil on linen
24 inch diameter

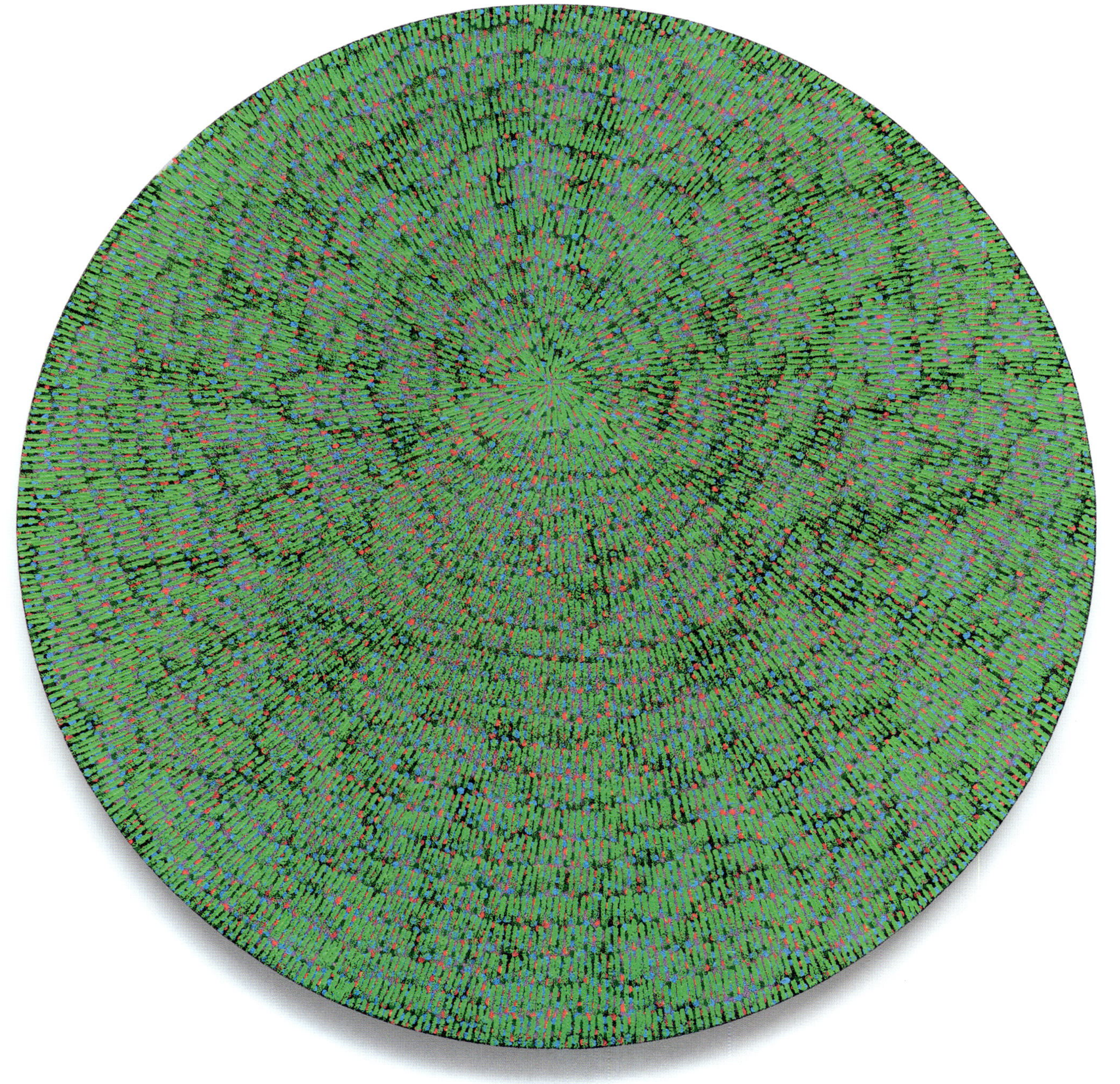

Lotus Wheel Ajna (Seven Chakras), 2022
Sand, acrylic and oil on linen
24 inch diameter

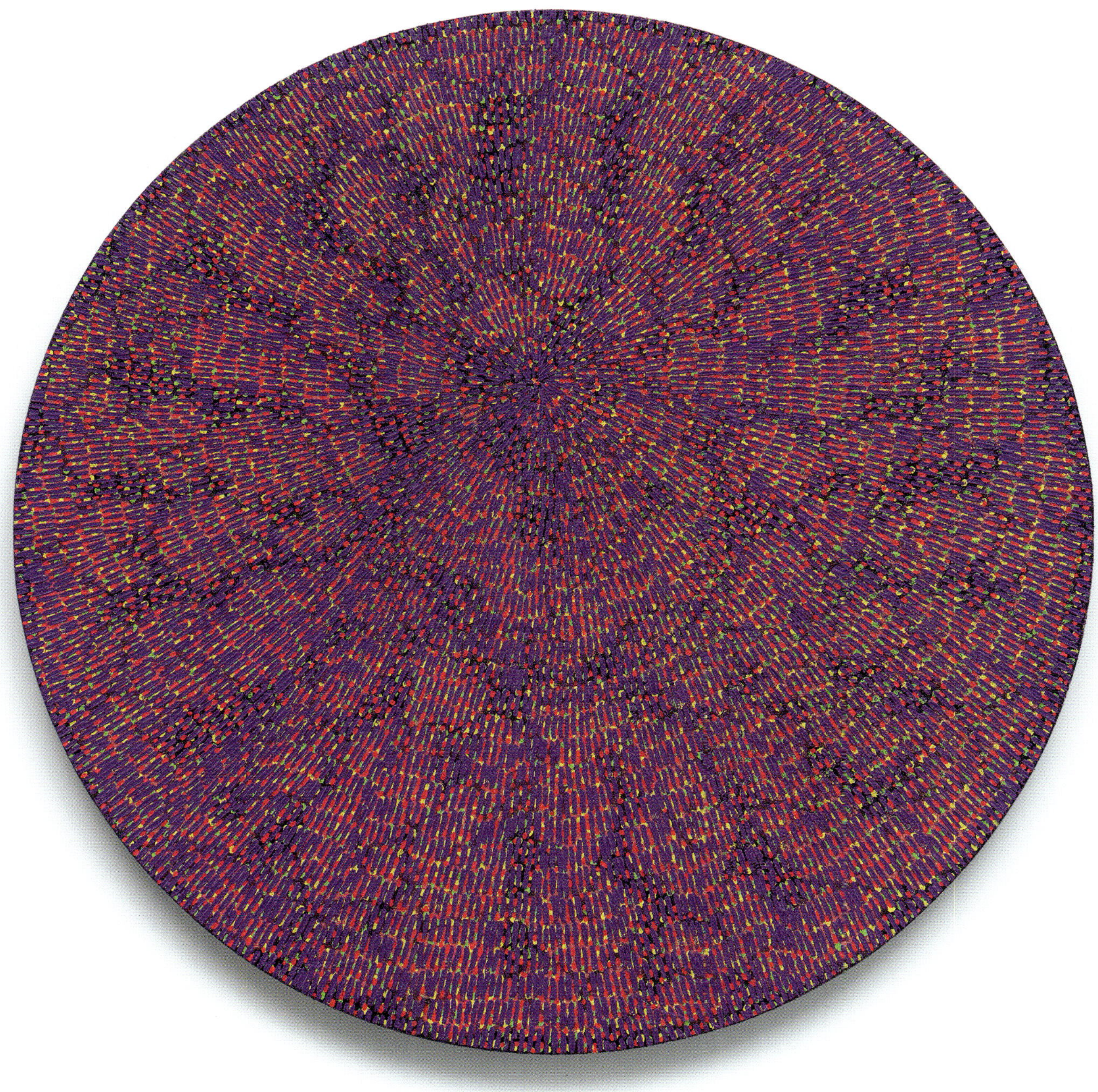

Lotus Wheel Muladhara
(Seven Chakras), 2022
Sand, acrylic and oil on linen
24 inch diameter

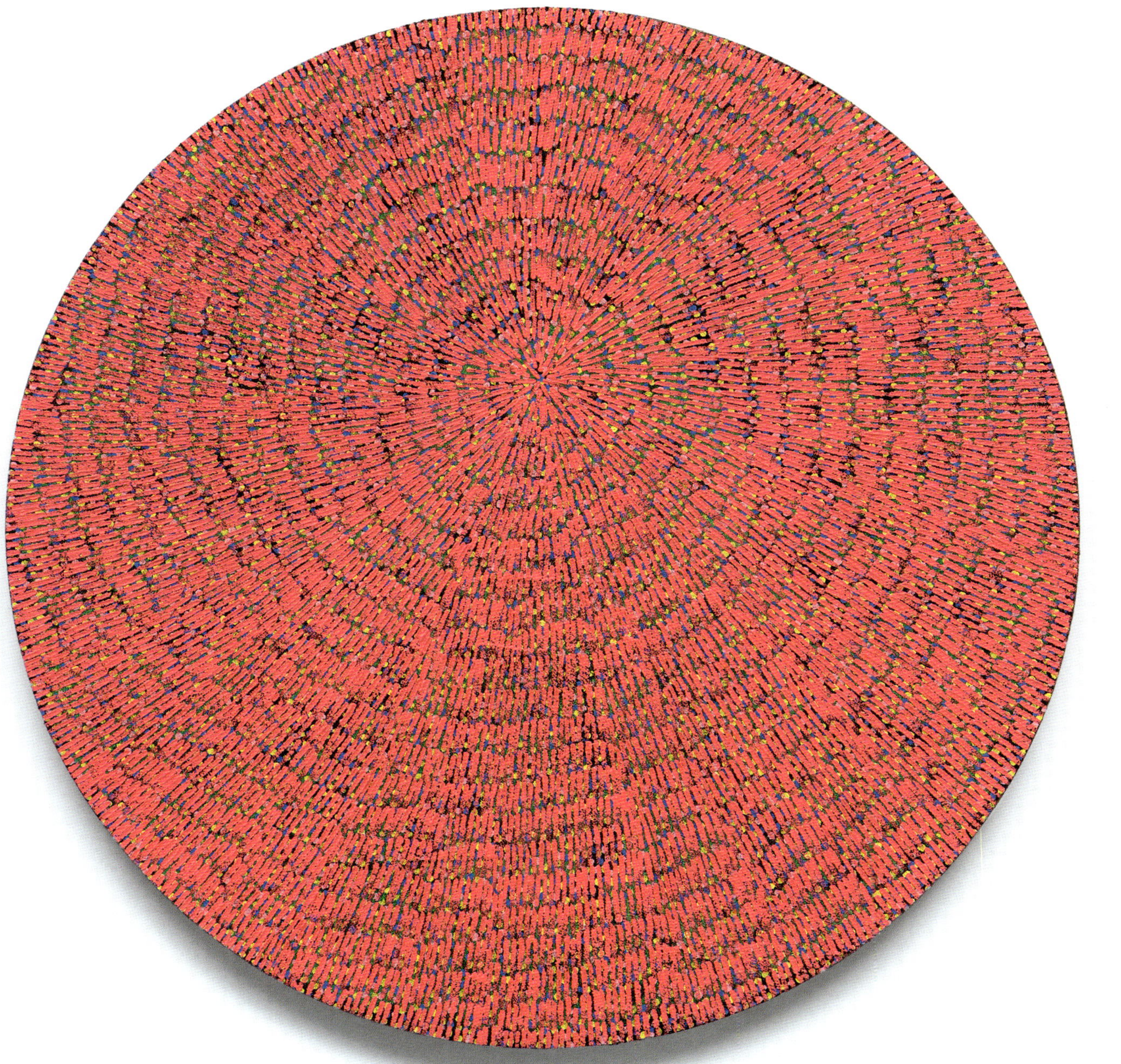

Lotus Wheel Vishuddha
(Seven Chakras), 2022
Sand, acrylic and oil on linen
24 inch diameter

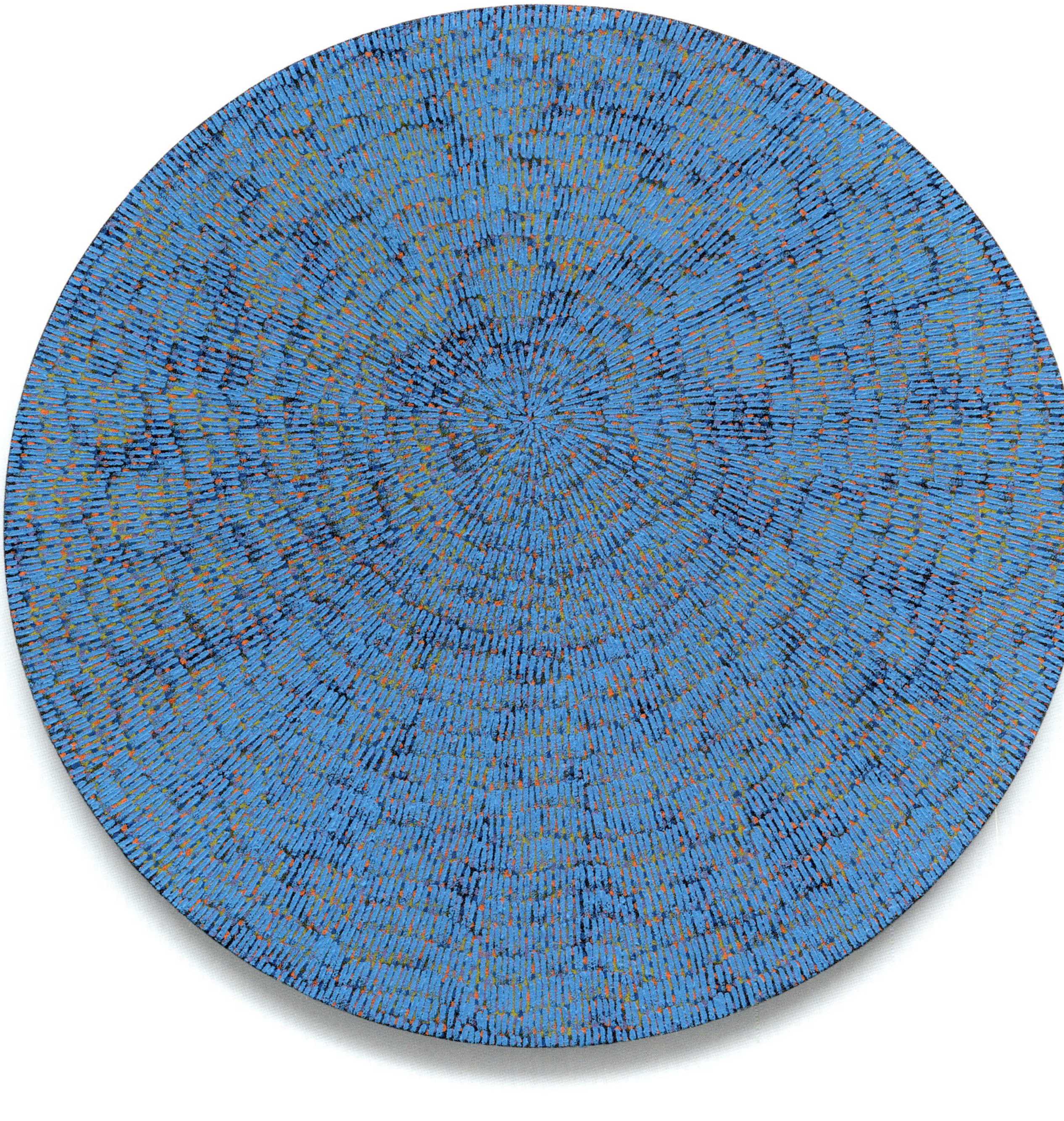

Lotus Wheel Swadhisthana (Seven Chakras), 2022
Sand, acrylic and oil on linen
24 inch diameter

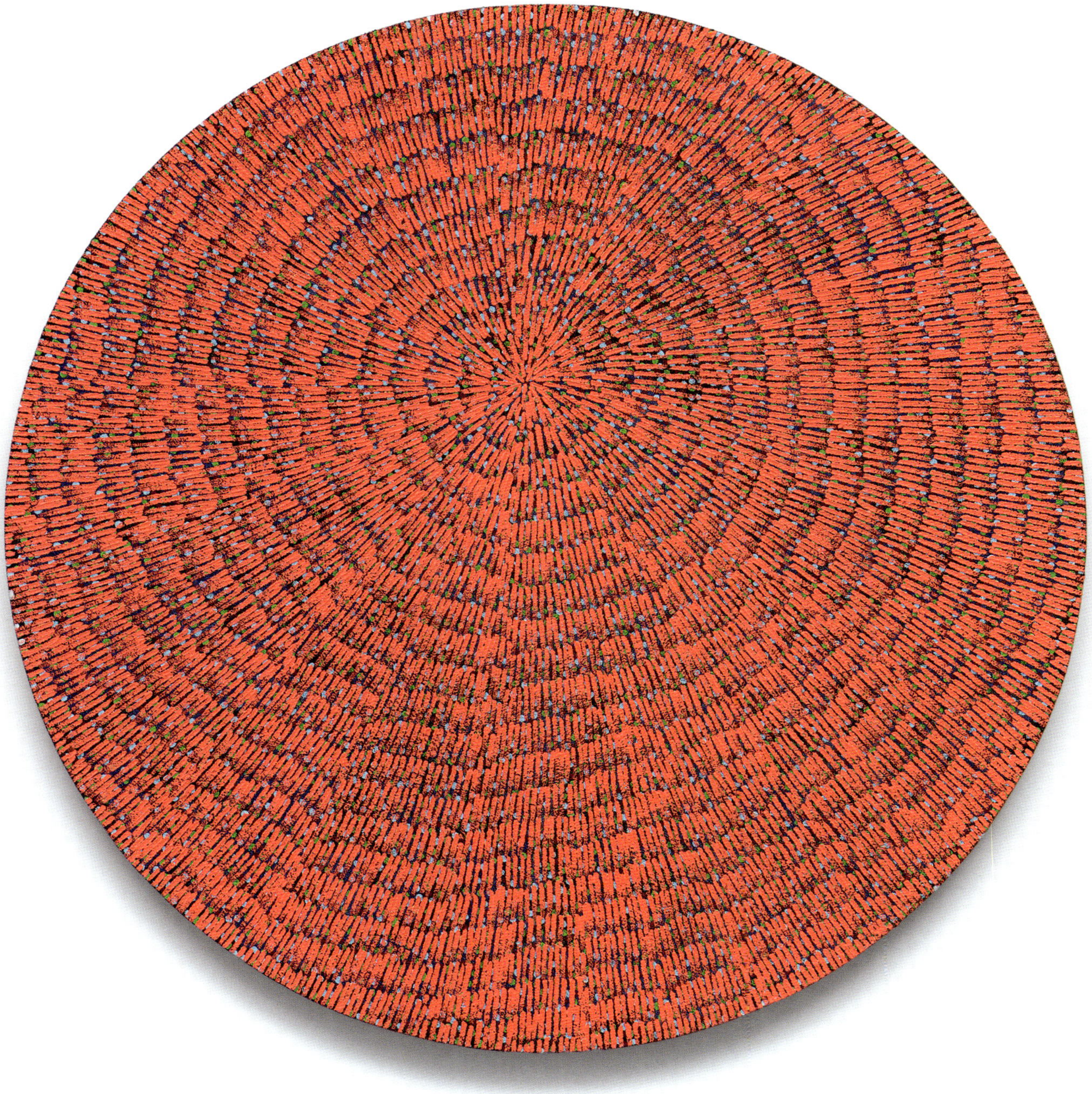

Capitol Creek B (Green Sand SF #2G Mandala, Green Ground), 2017
Sand and acrylic on linen
116 x 98 inches

Abundance and Harmony
(Painted White Sand, Orange and Blue,
Pink Ground), 2021
Sand, acrylic and oil on linen
34 x 27 inches

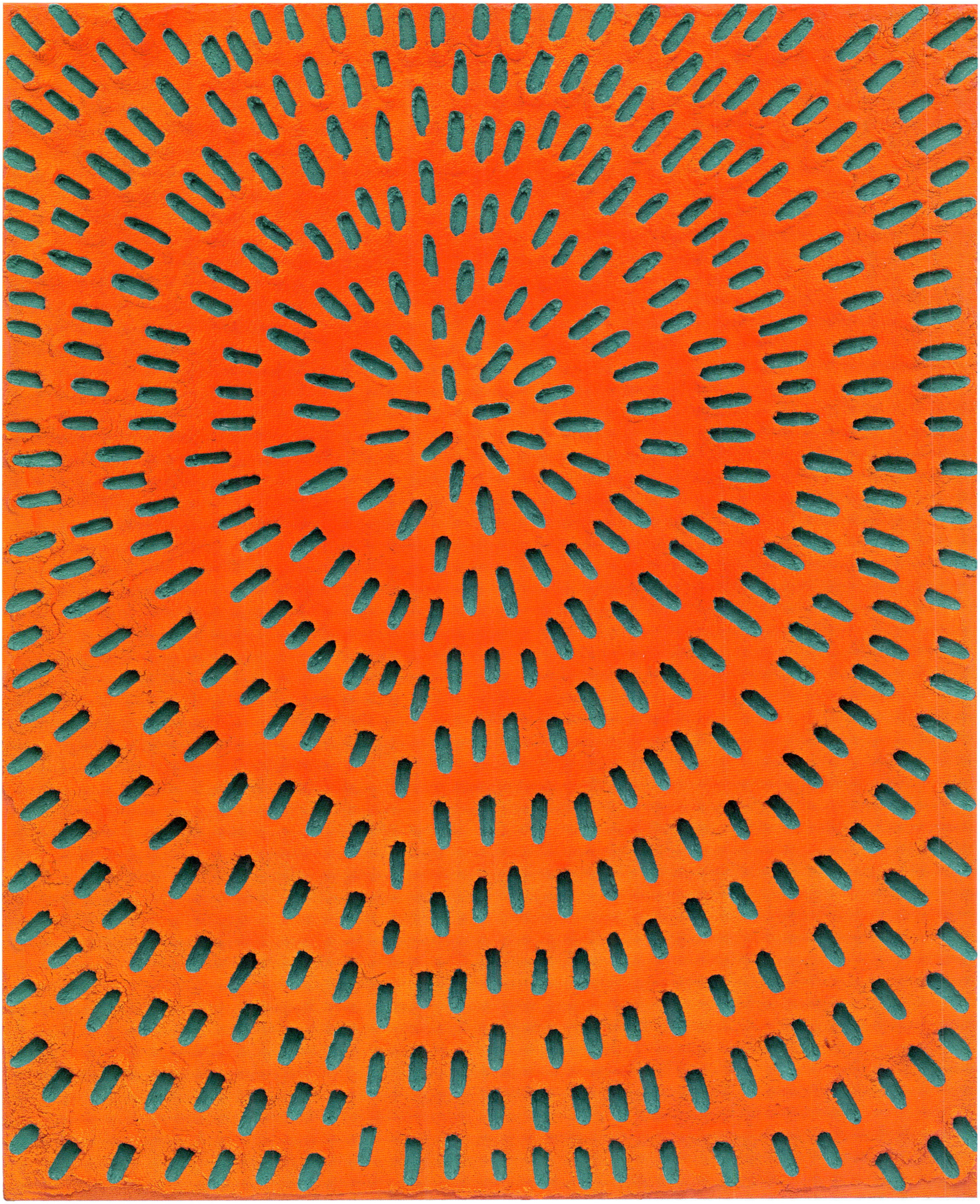

No Words Just Stars
(Hot Pink #1PT, Black Sand SF #1C), 2017
Sand, acrylic and oil on linen
41 x 35 inches

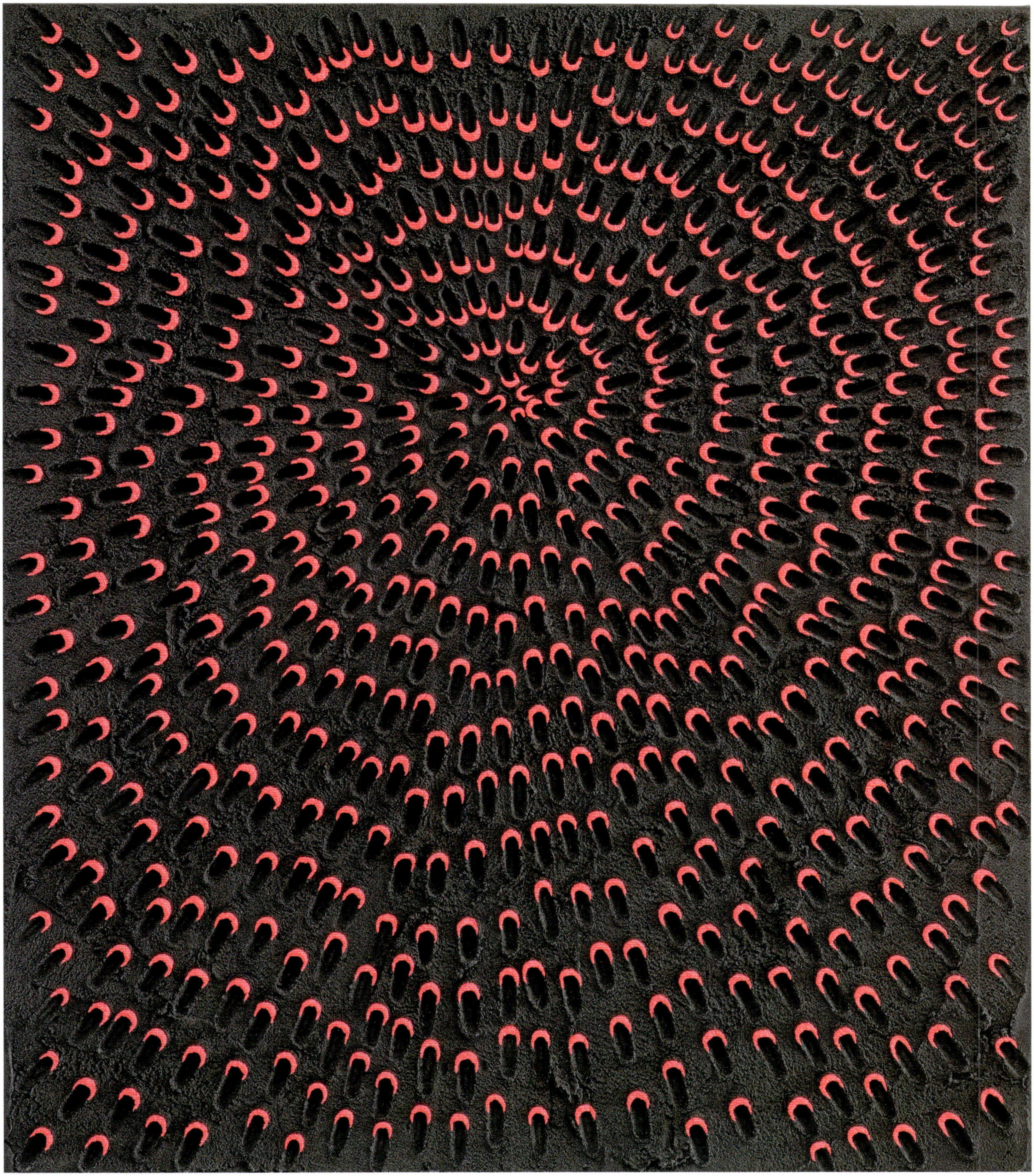

Emblazoned Sky (Painted Purple Sand, Pink-Orange-Yellow Gradient, Blue, Purple Ground), 2021
Sand, acrylic and oil on linen
21 x 15 inches

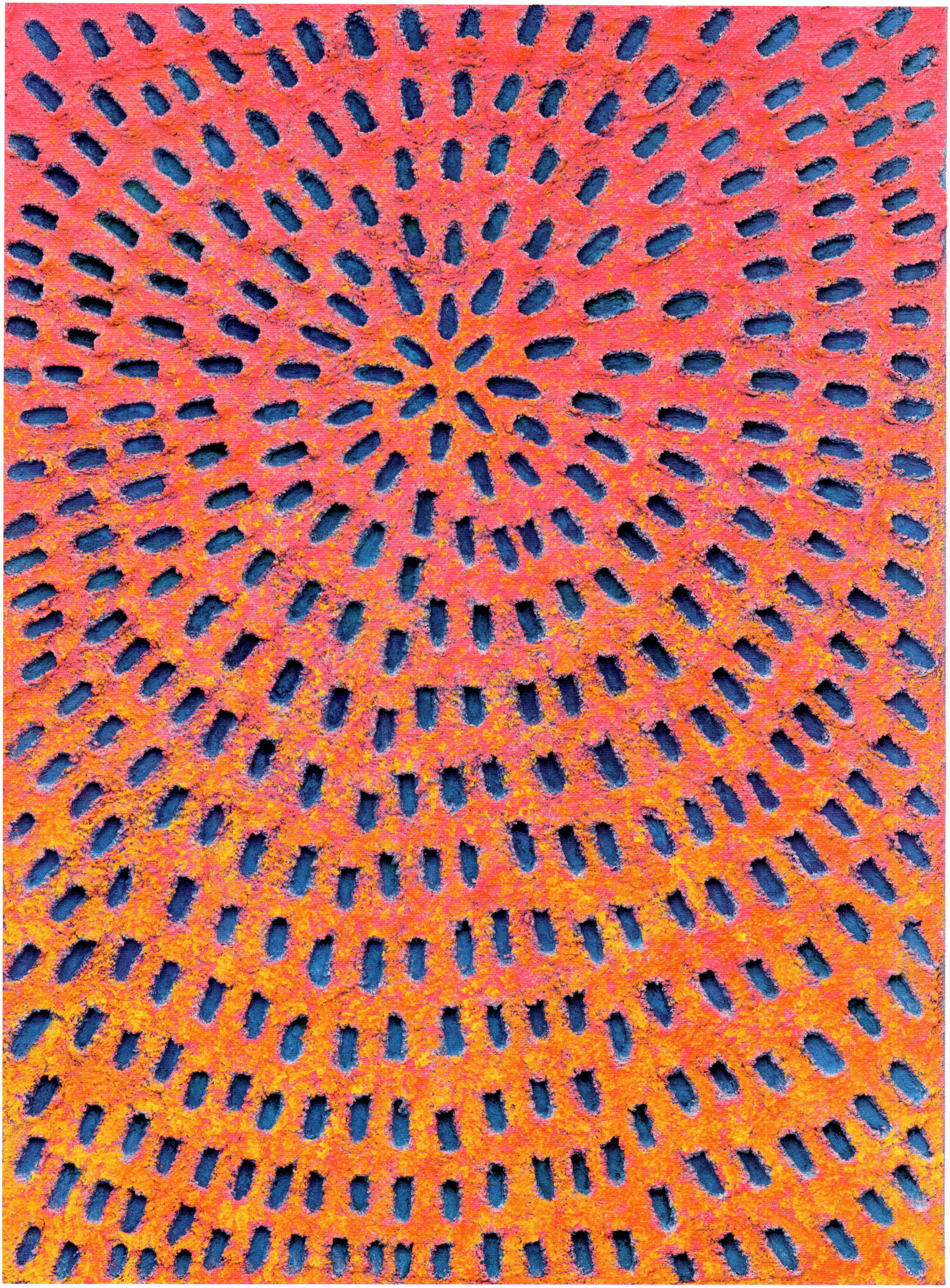

Sweetness of Life (Painted White Sand, Green and Pink, Pink Ground), 2021
Sand, acrylic and oil on linen
34 x 27 inches

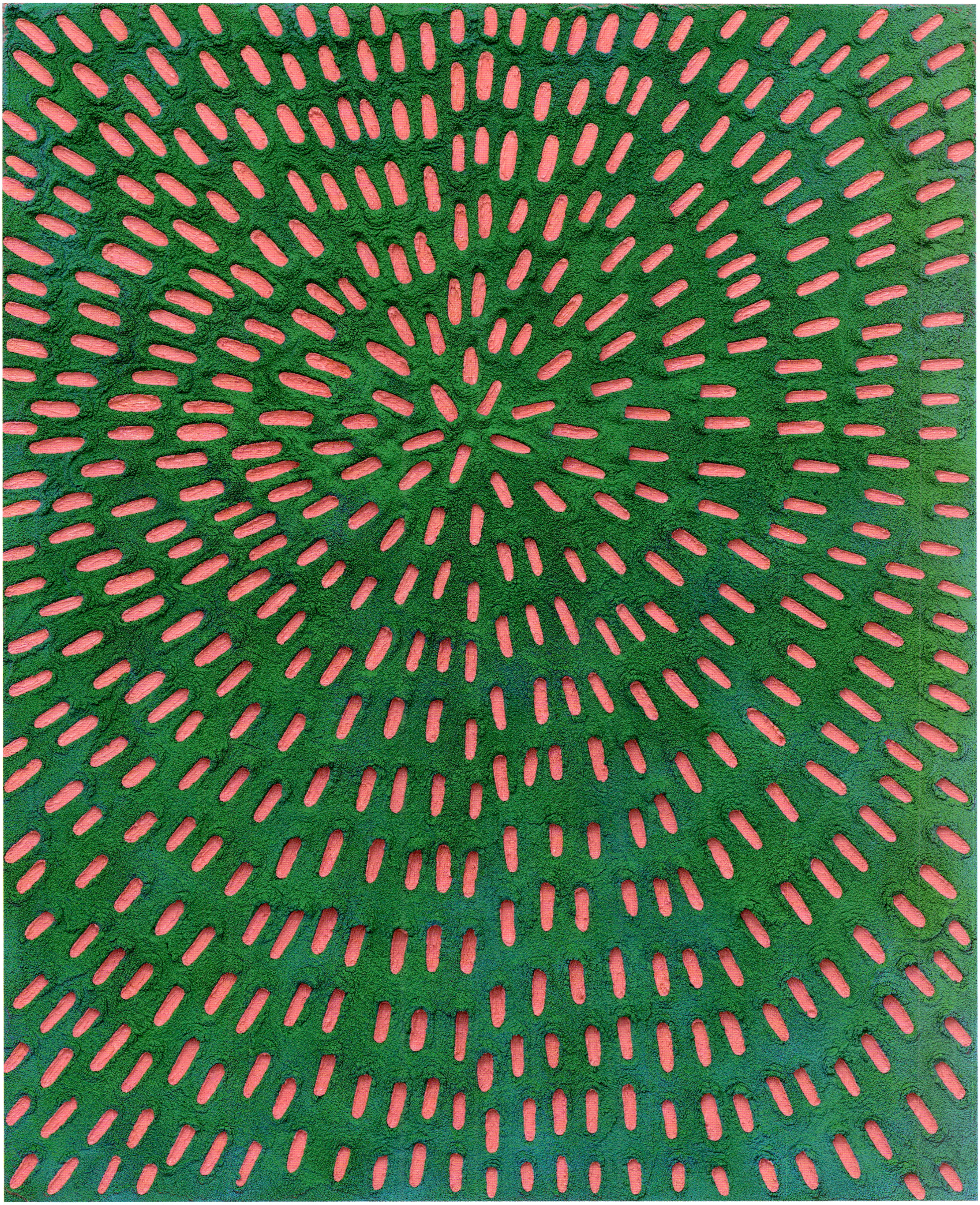

Points of Connection (Painted Blue Sand, Light Blue, Green and Blue, Blue Ground), 2020
Sand, acrylic and oil on linen
21 x 15 inches

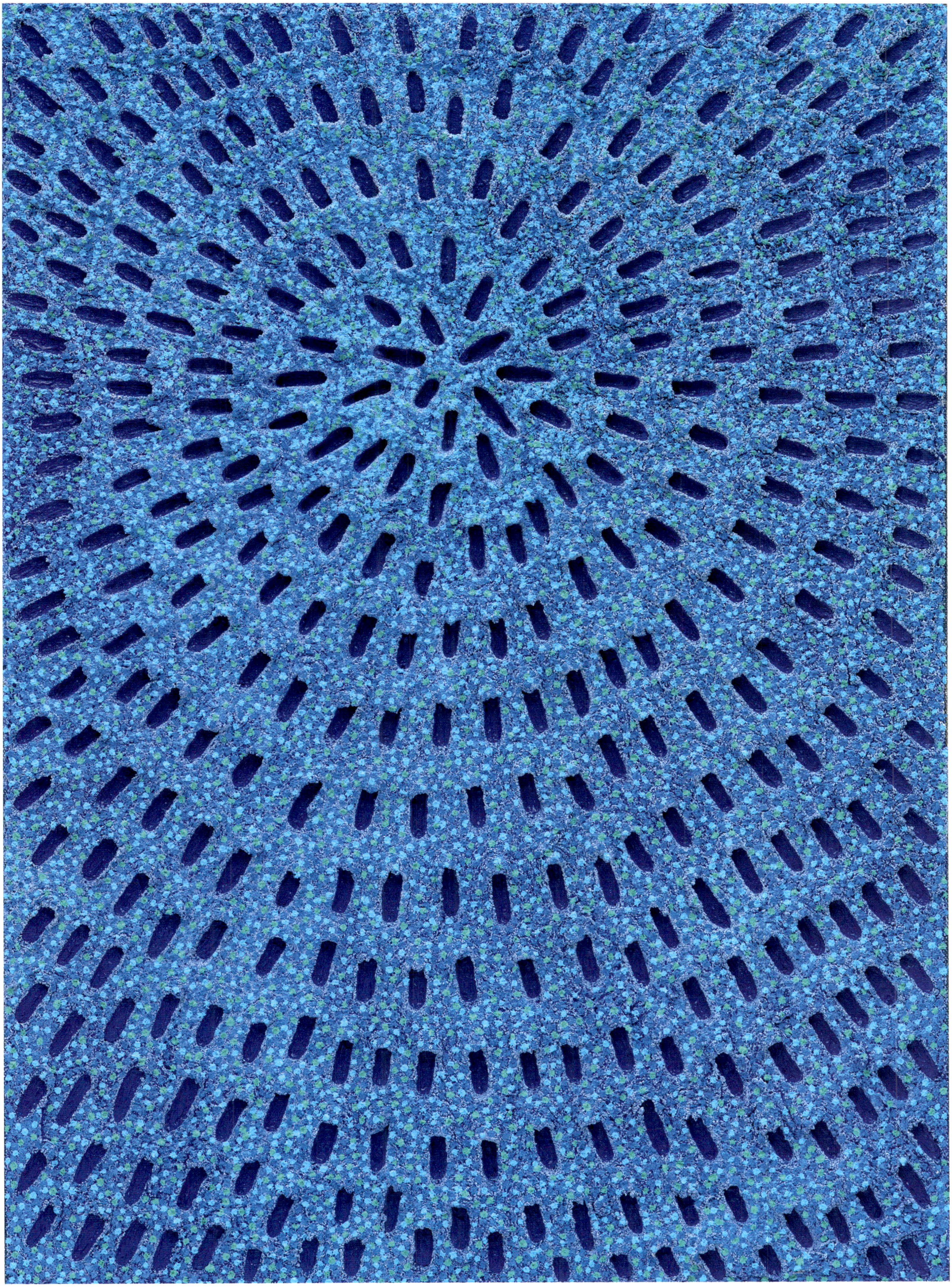

Wave of Blessings (Red PT, Turquoise, Painted Pink Sand, Yellow), 2022
Sand, acrylic and oil on linen
21 x 15 inches

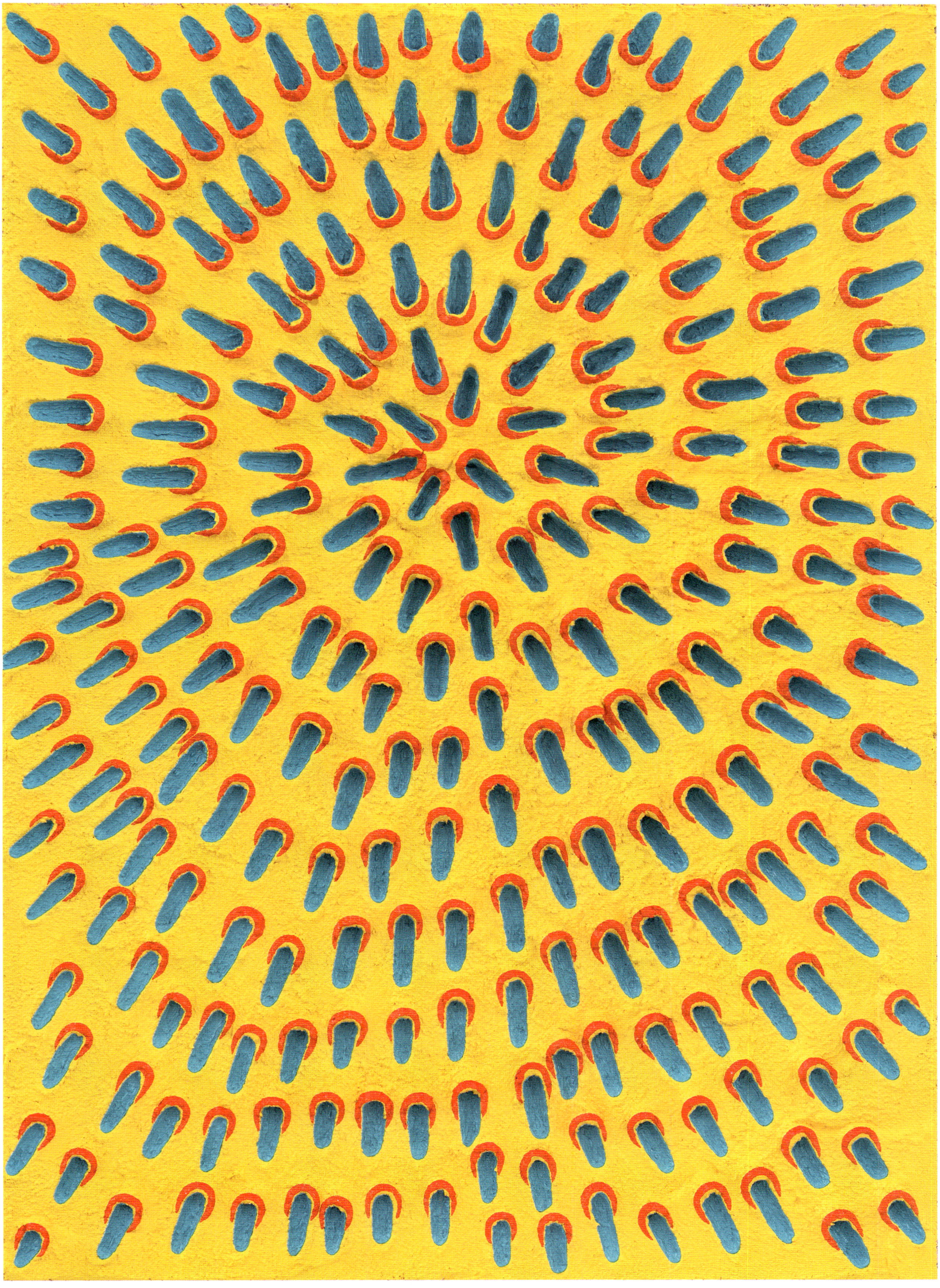

Petals to the Sun (Painted White Sand, Red-Pink-Orange-Yellow Gradient, Lavender Center), 2021
Sand, acrylic and oil on linen
21 x 15 inches

Petals to the Sun combines research on gesture and mandalas to create a two-dimensional sculpture in which light and texture coexist, revealing kaleidoscopic tonal effects and attractions. The rich surface texture is the result of the artist's inquisitive creative process, which involves sand mixed with acrylic paint distributed across the canvas. On the damp surface, using special tools, several indentations are pushed into the sand mixture radiating from a central point to create concentric forms. Once the sculptural form is hardened, Guidi creates new layers in oil paint, and with each refined tone of color and the space it inhabits, Guidi's works unleash complex sensory experiences.

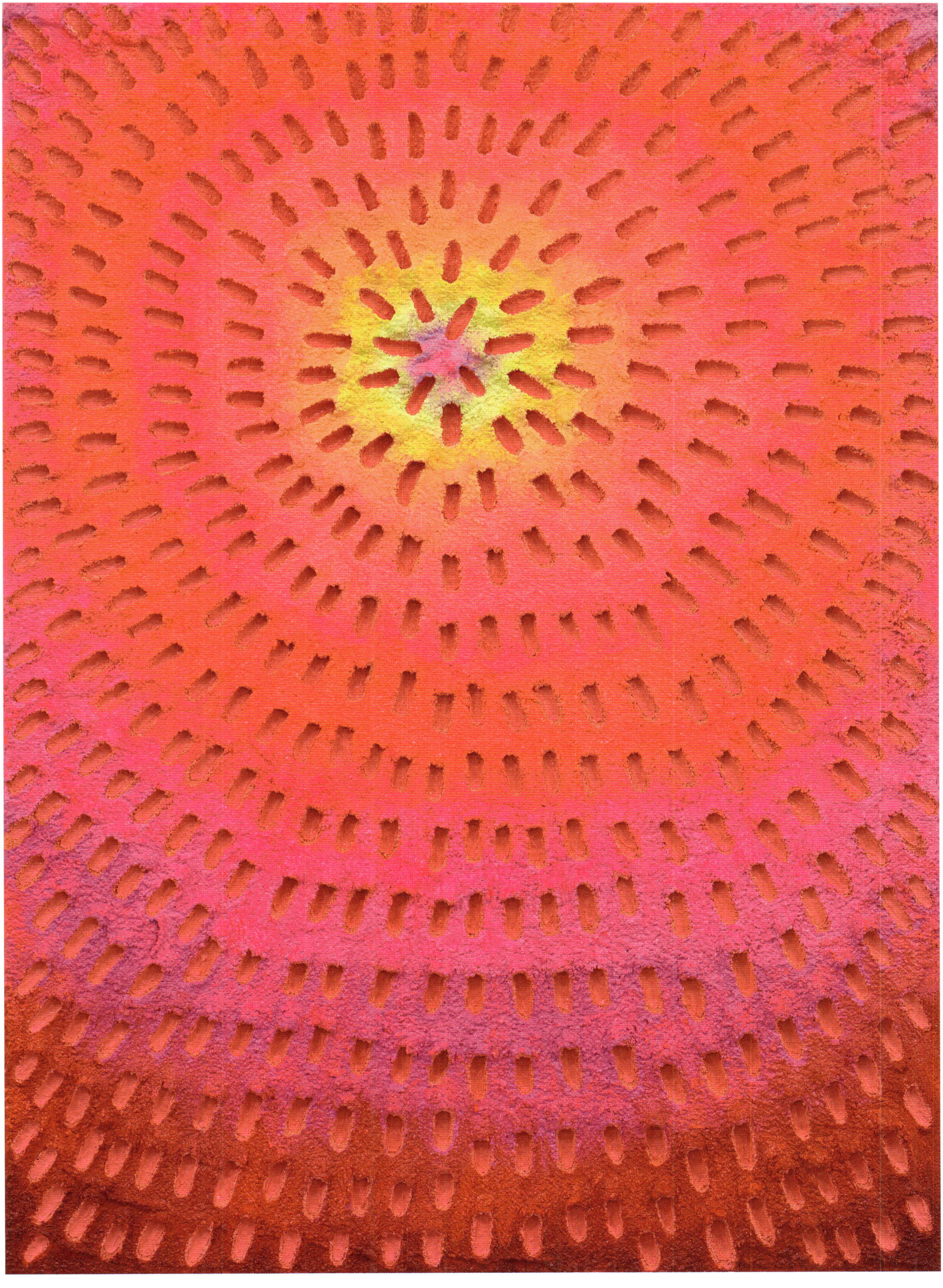

Misty Morning (Painted White Sand, Green-Blue Gradient, Green, Green Ground), 2021
Sand, acrylic and oil on linen
34 x 27 inches

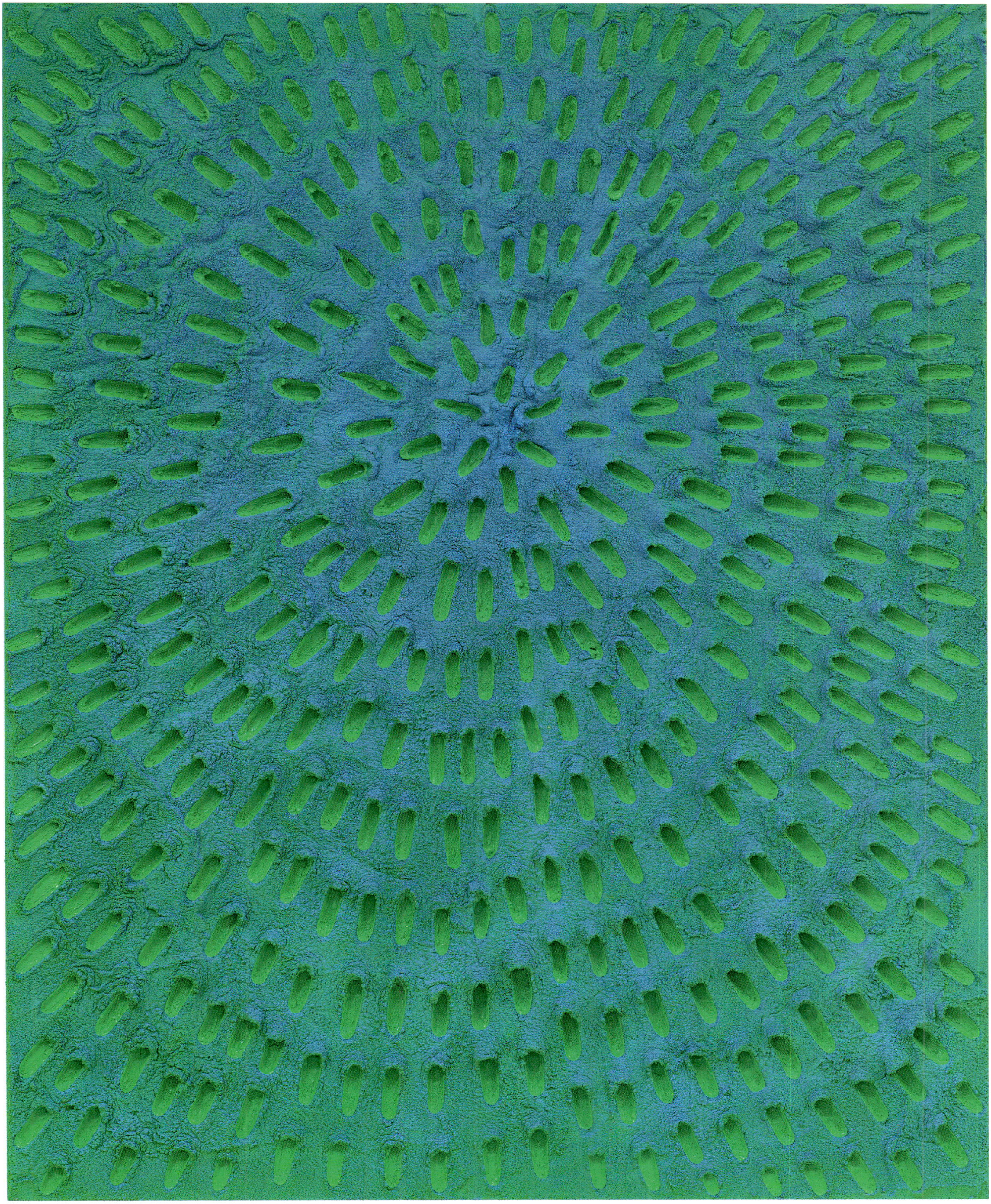

Fully Illuminated (Painted White Sand, Multicolor, Light Blue Ground), 2021
Sand, acrylic and oil on linen
34 x 27 inches

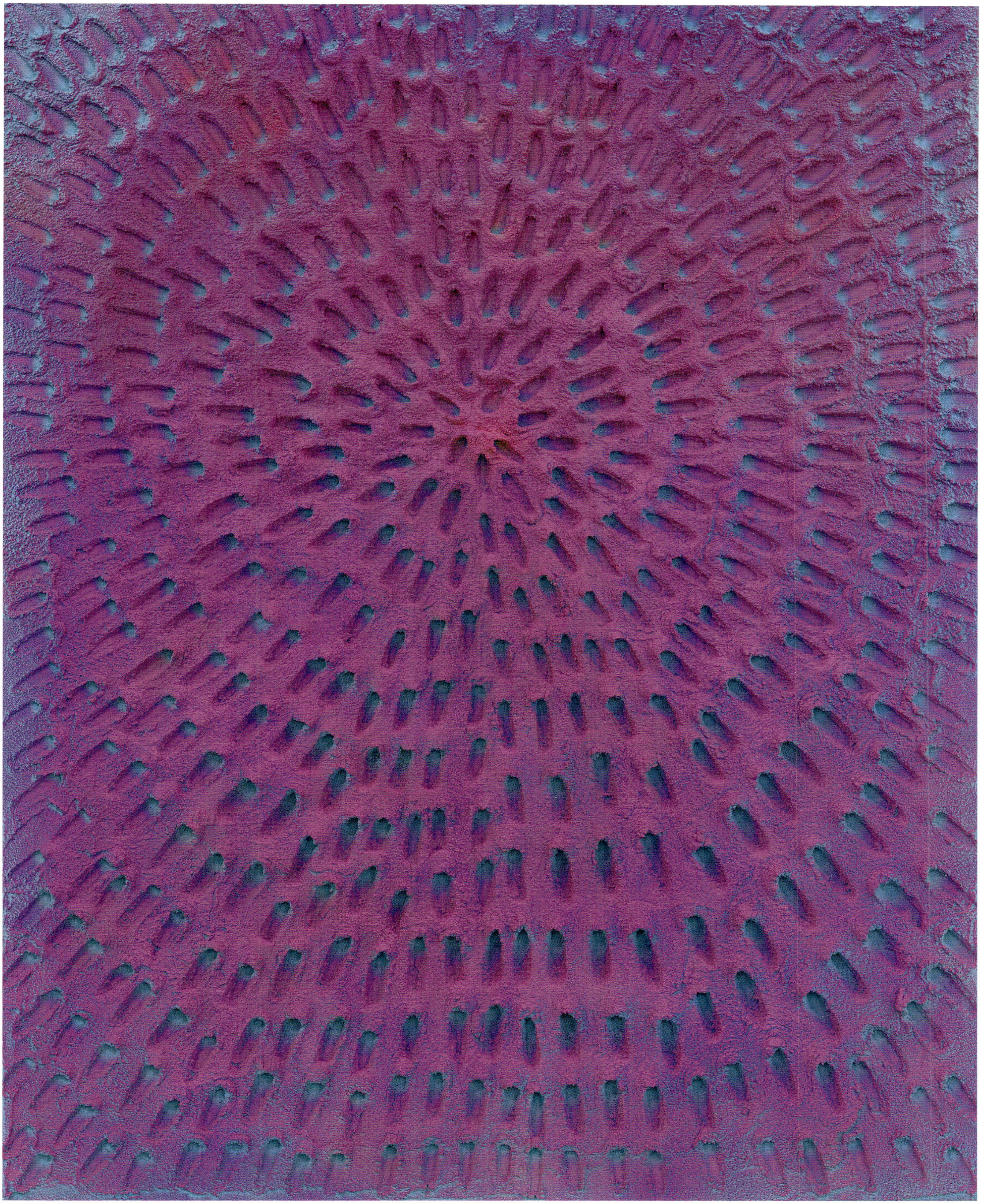

Immersed in Inner Peace (Painted Universe Mandala, Light Blue, Yellow, Red and Pink, Natural Ground), 2021
Sand, acrylic and oil on linen
60 x 48 inches

Distinguished by Turner-esque color virtuosity, Guidi visualizes inner processes and experiences, describing these as precisely as possible to develop a unique expressive language in the painted universe mandala. Illustrative of Guidi's explorations of the painted surface and its texture, the sand-painting reflects the optical vibration and the artist's deep understanding of color and light, and their effect on the observer.

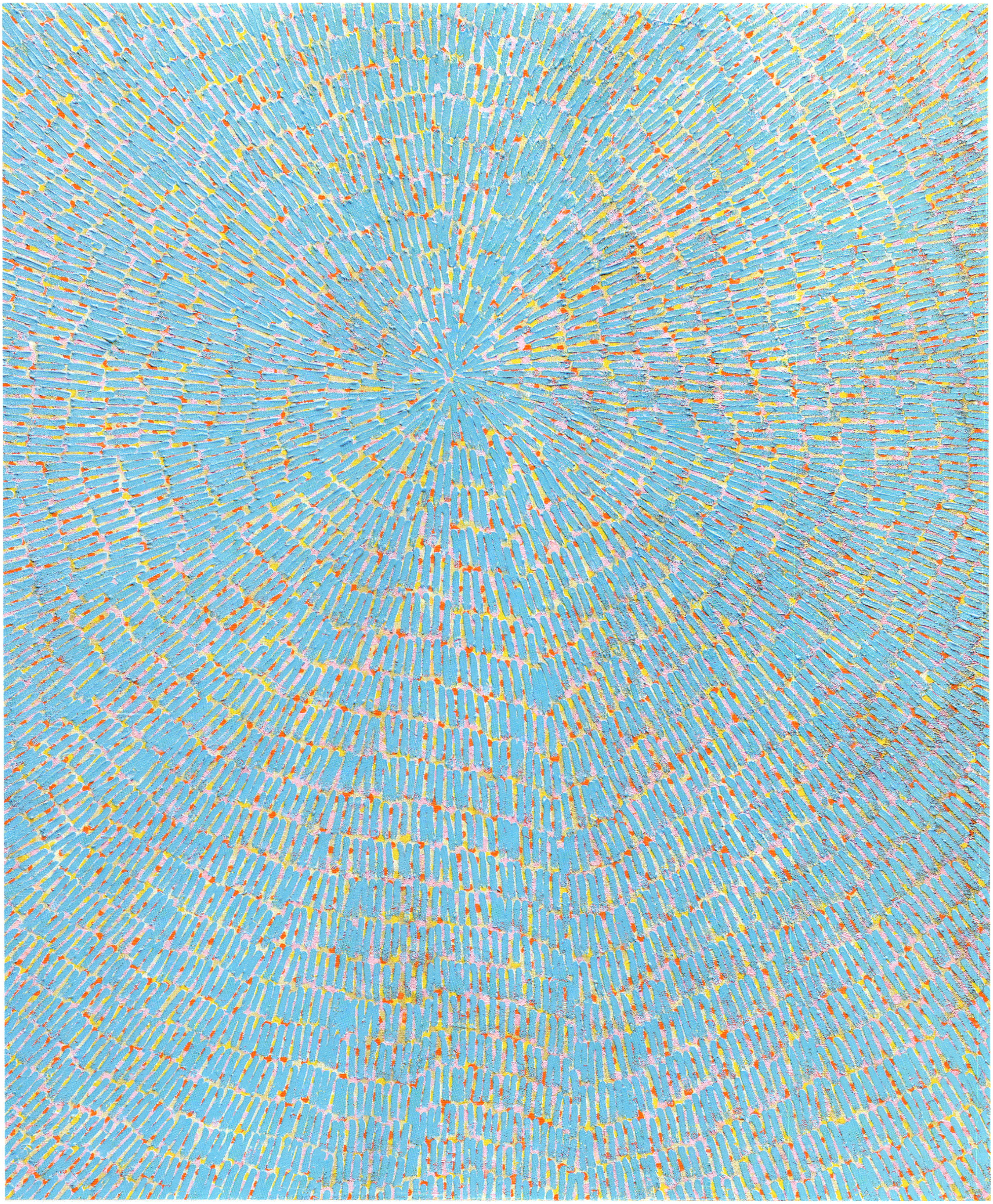

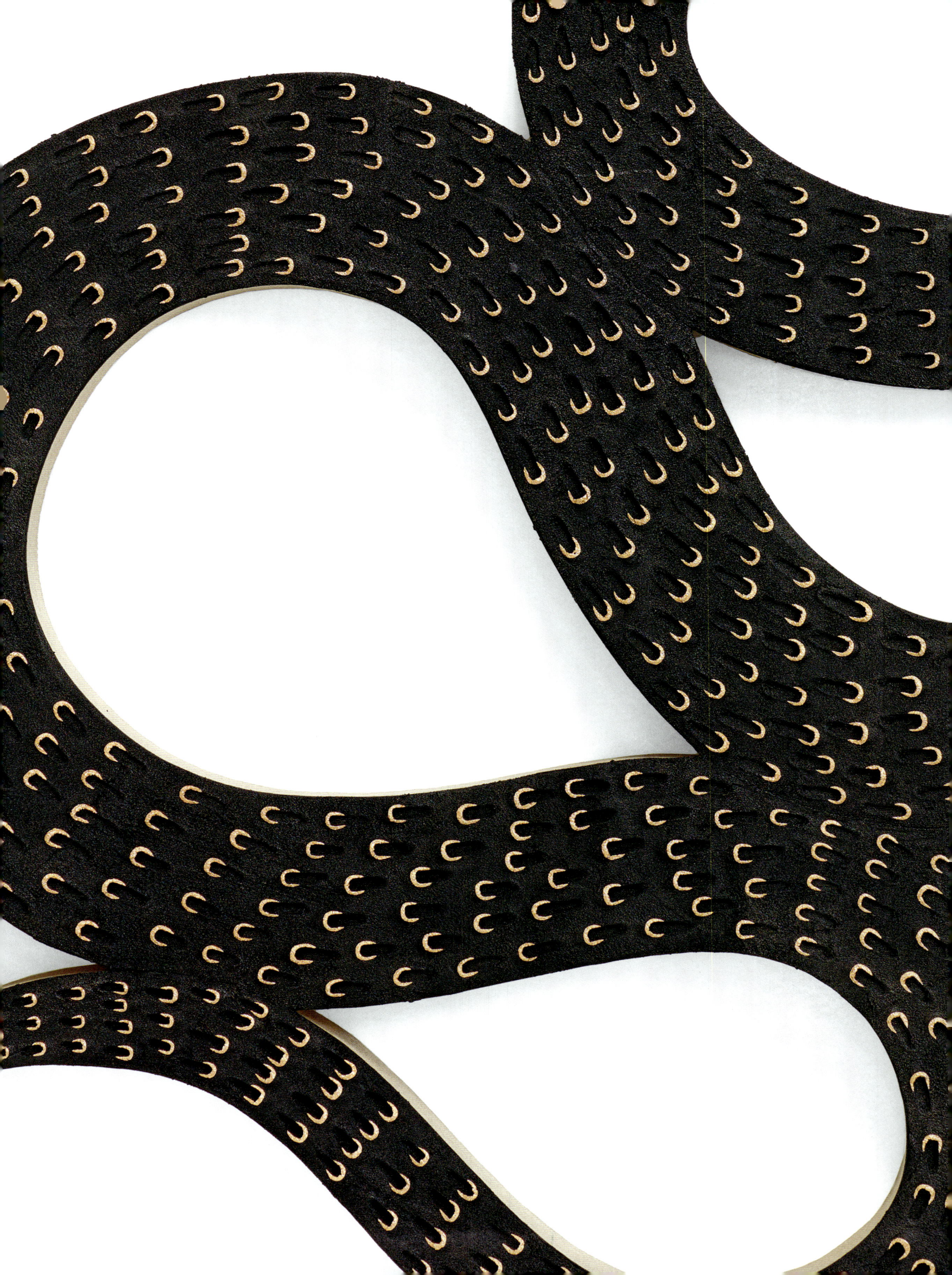

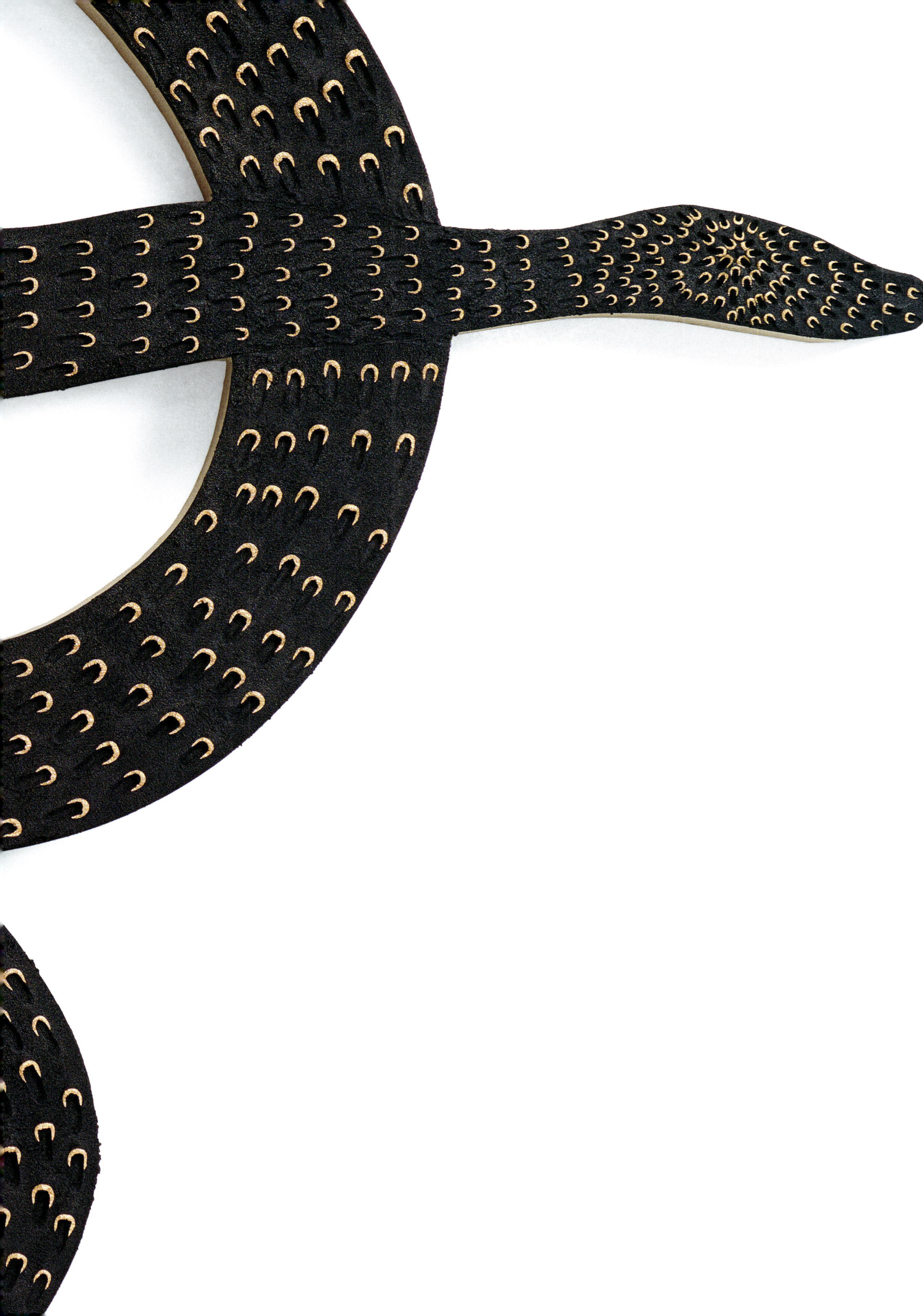

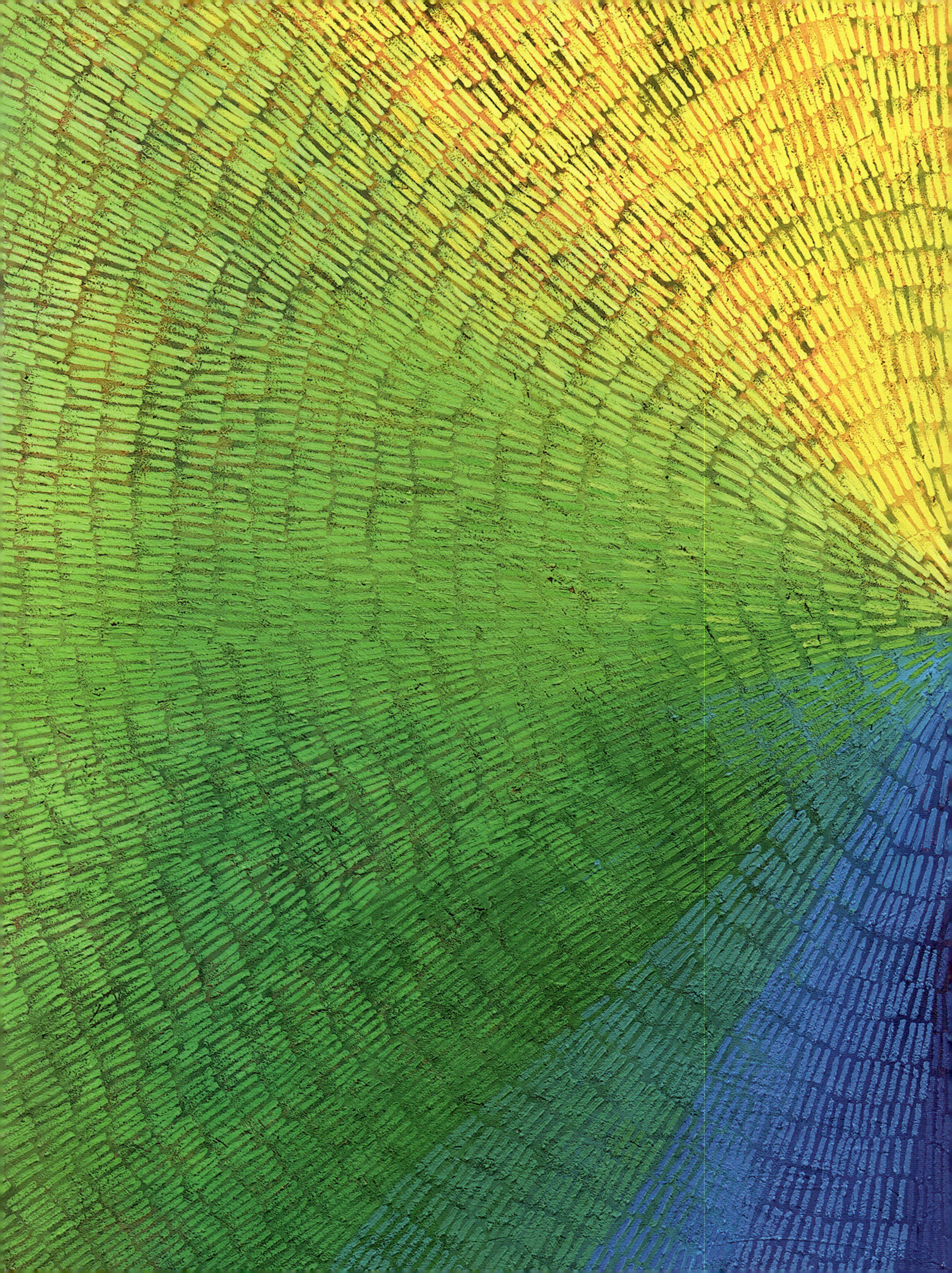

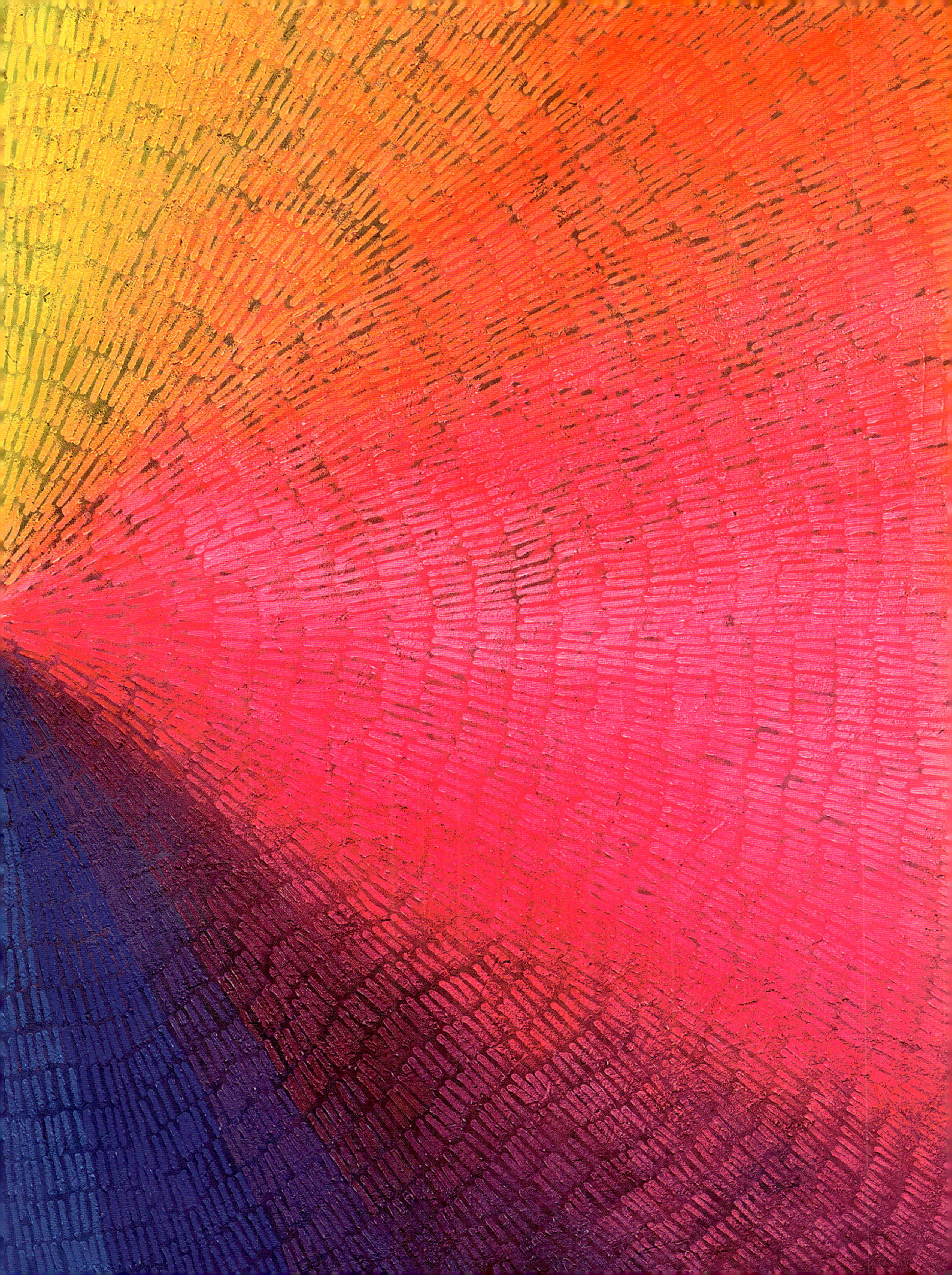

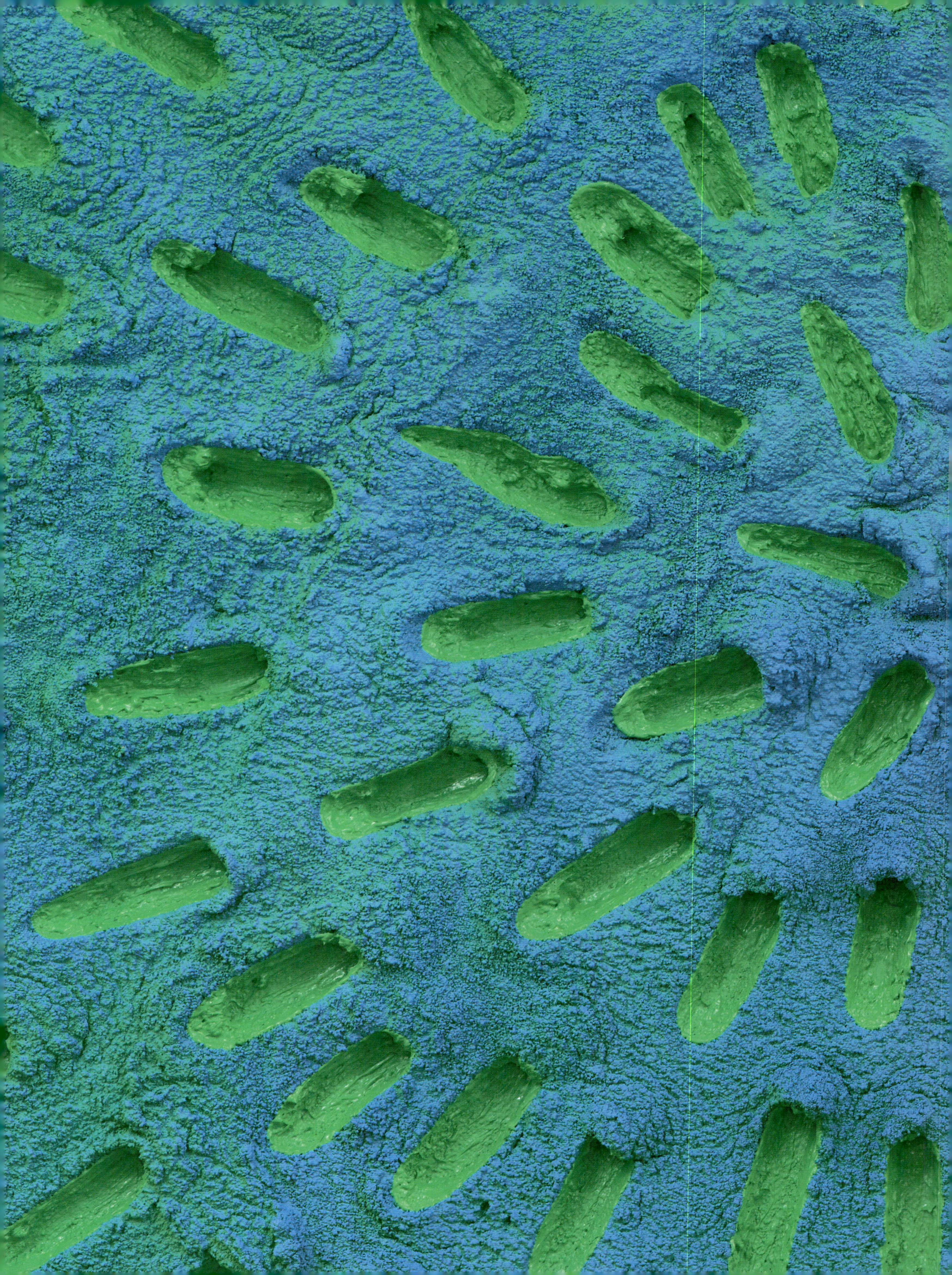

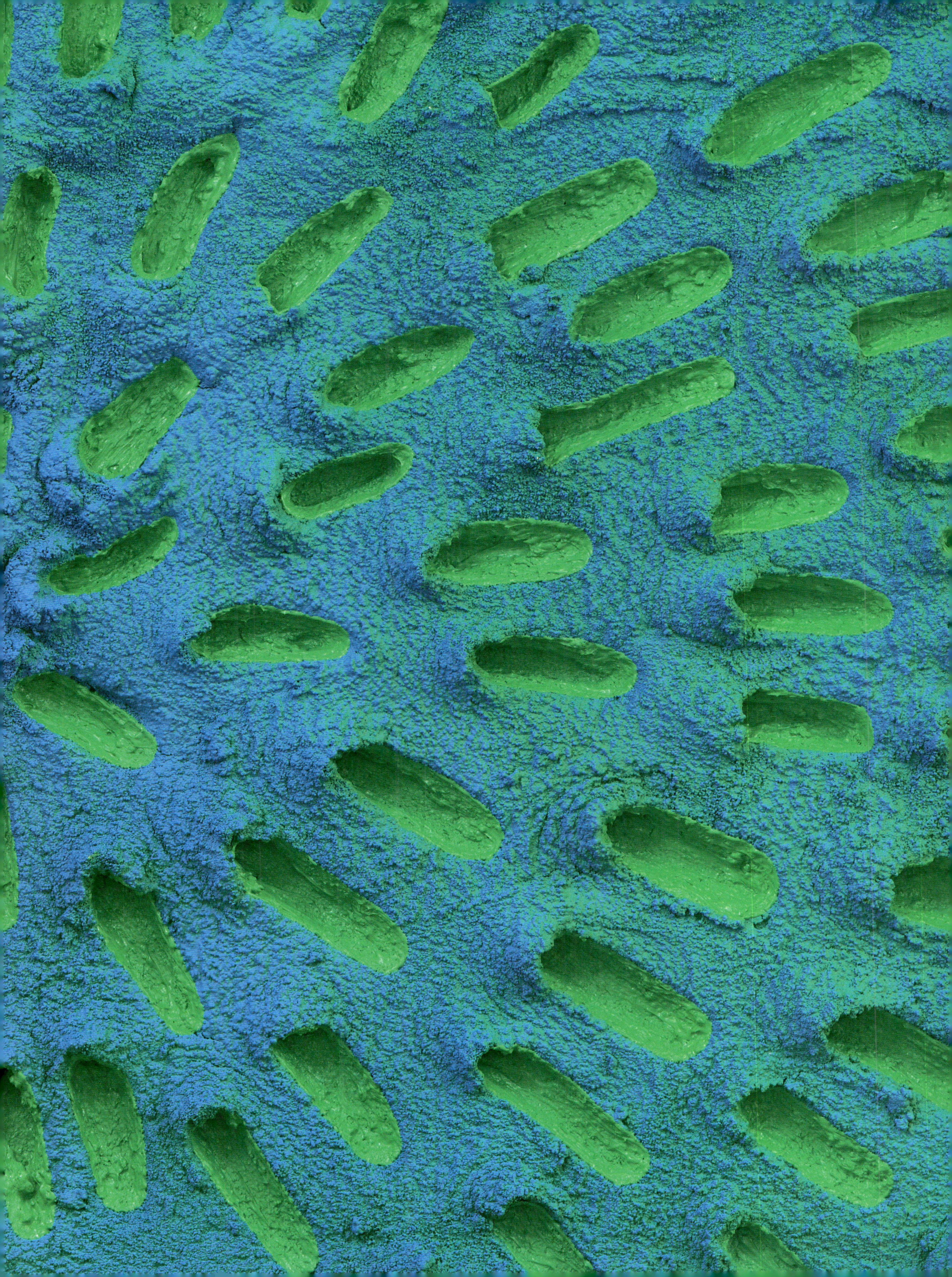

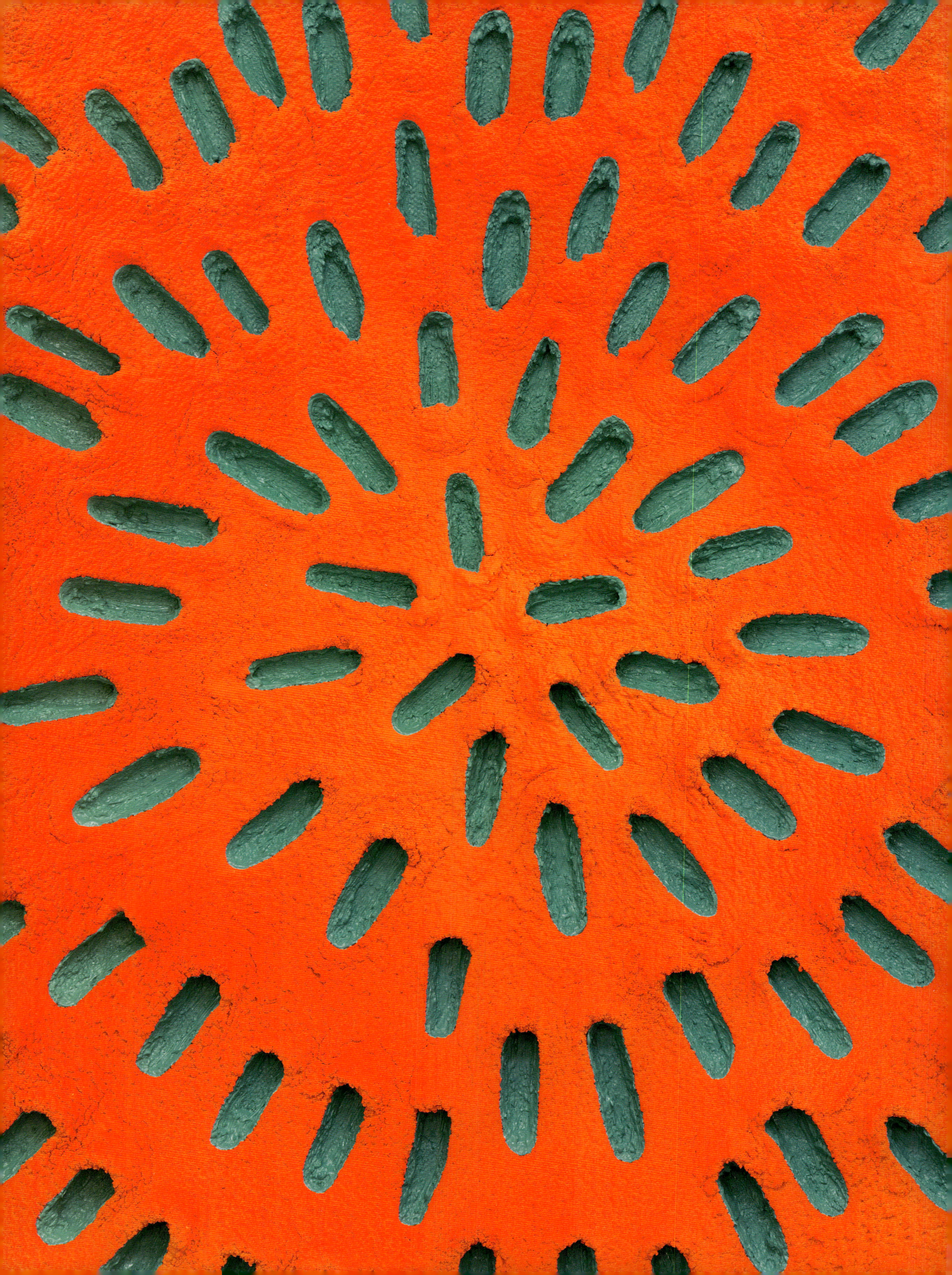

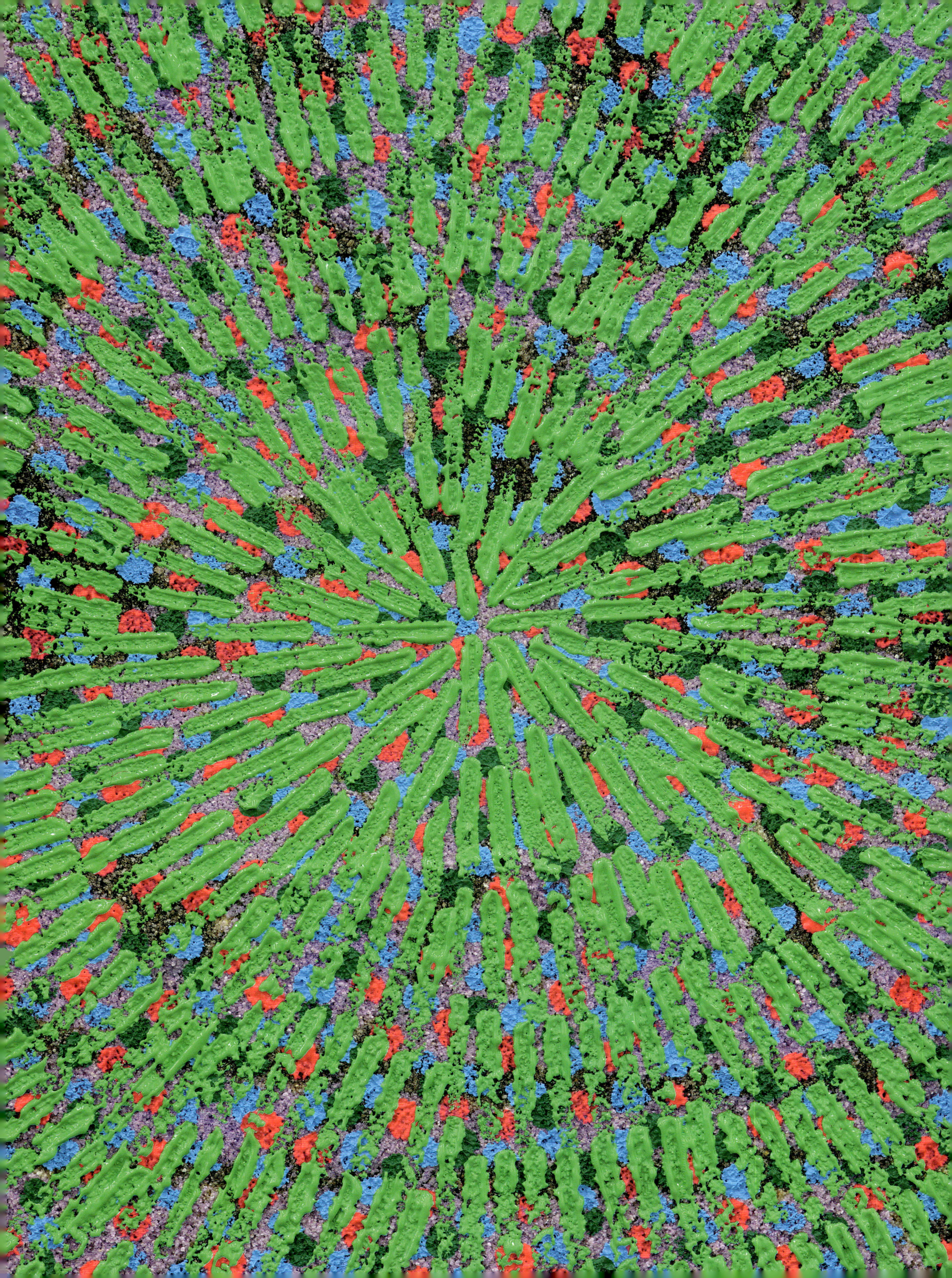

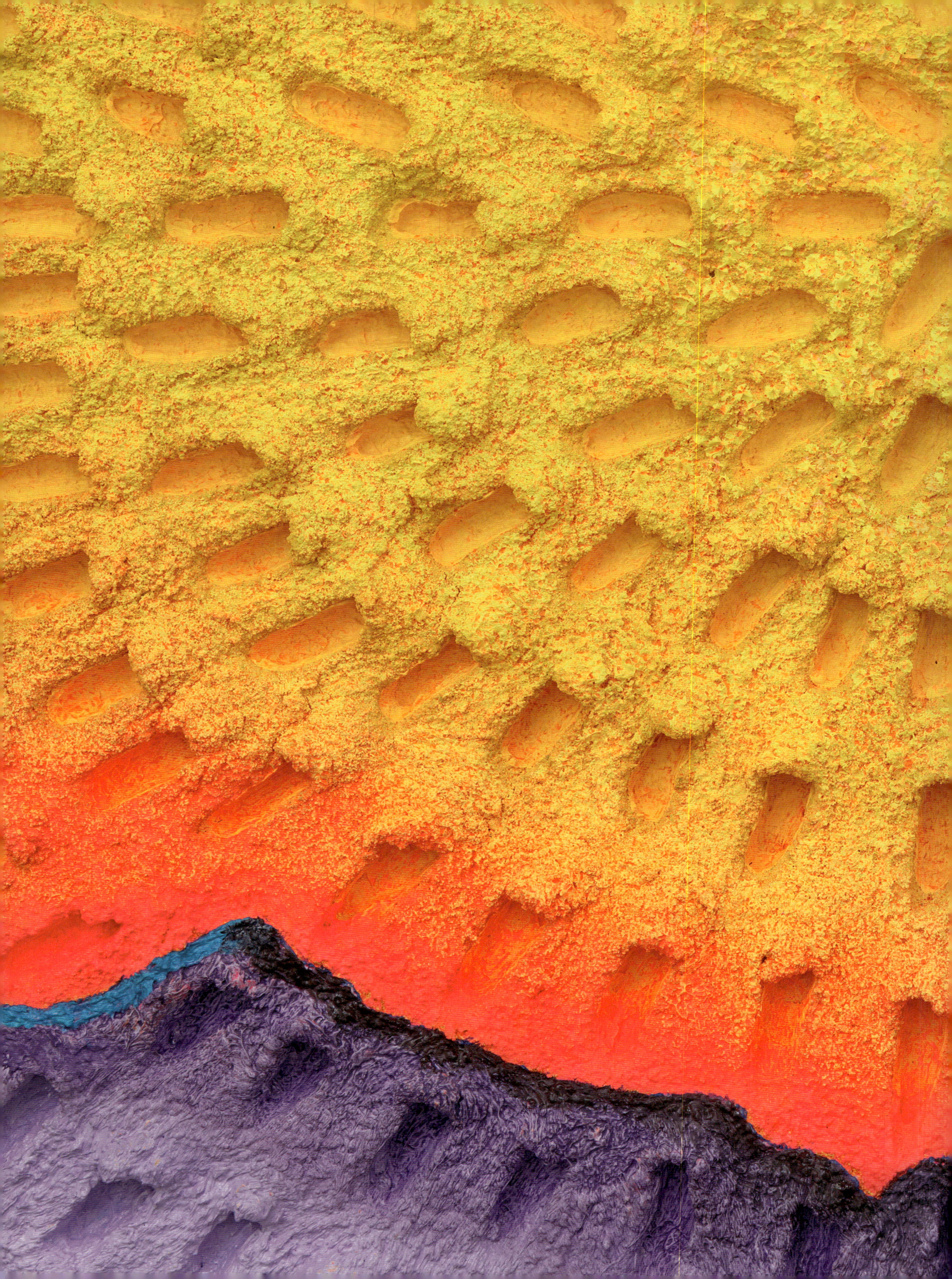

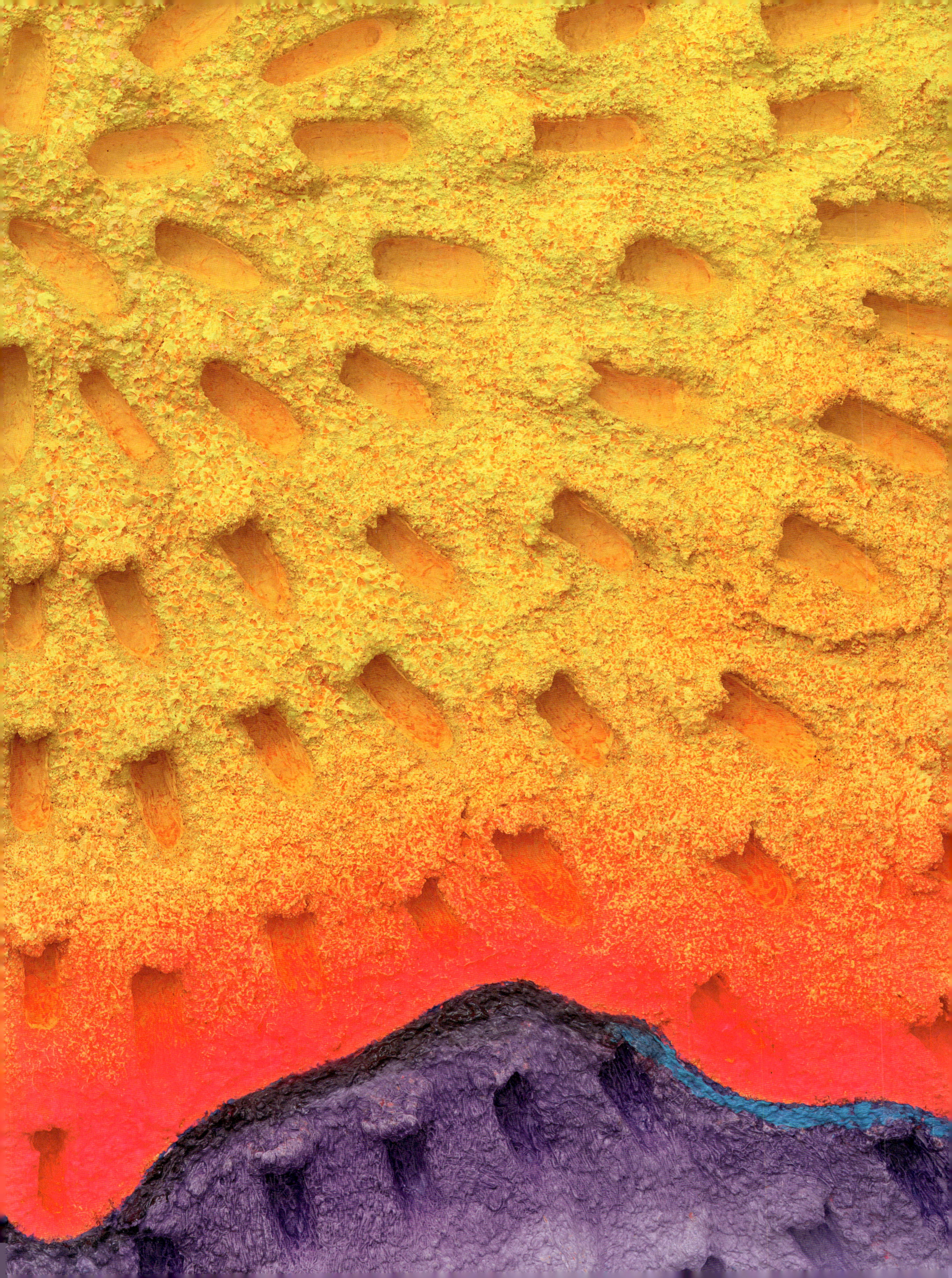

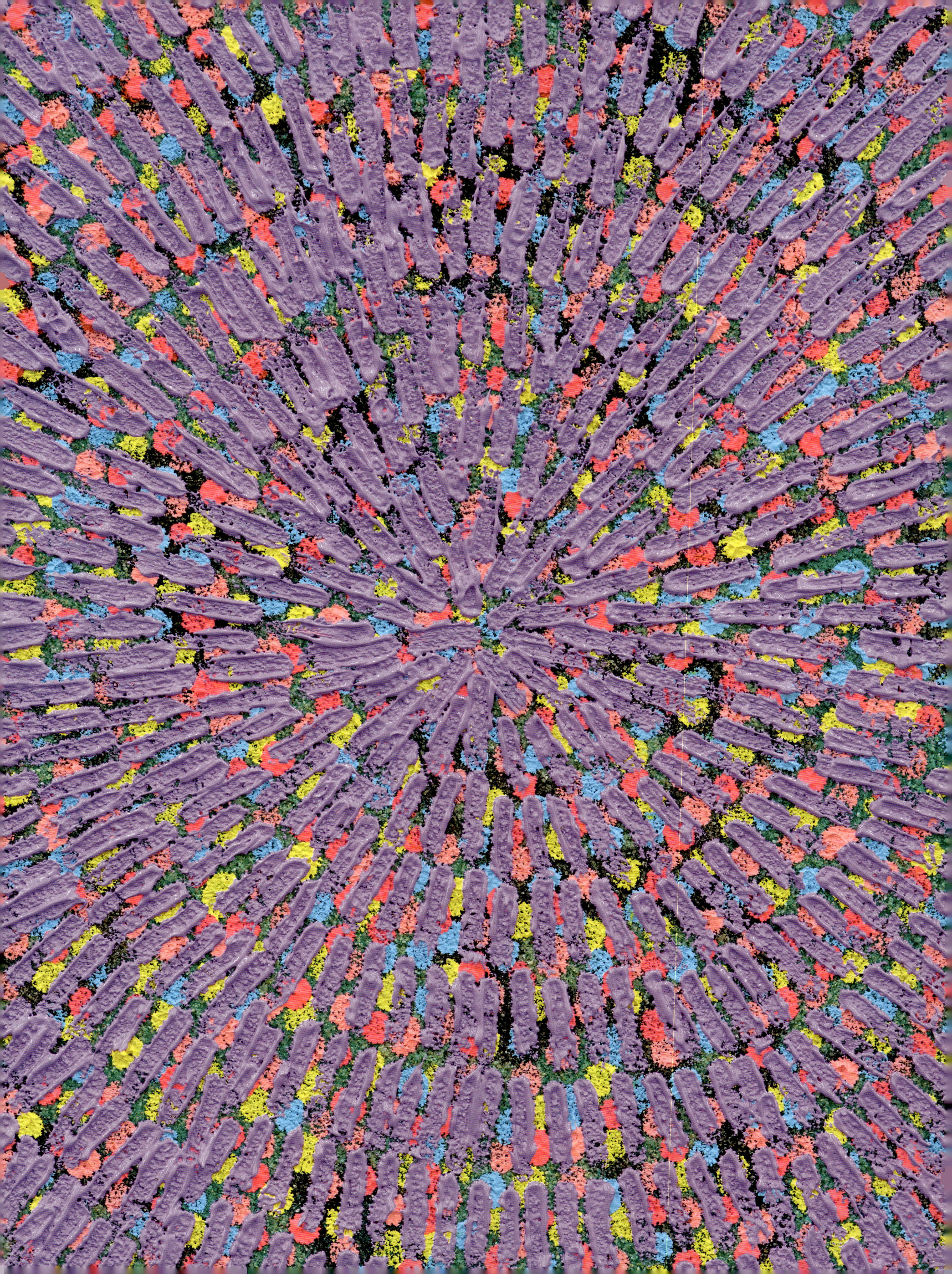

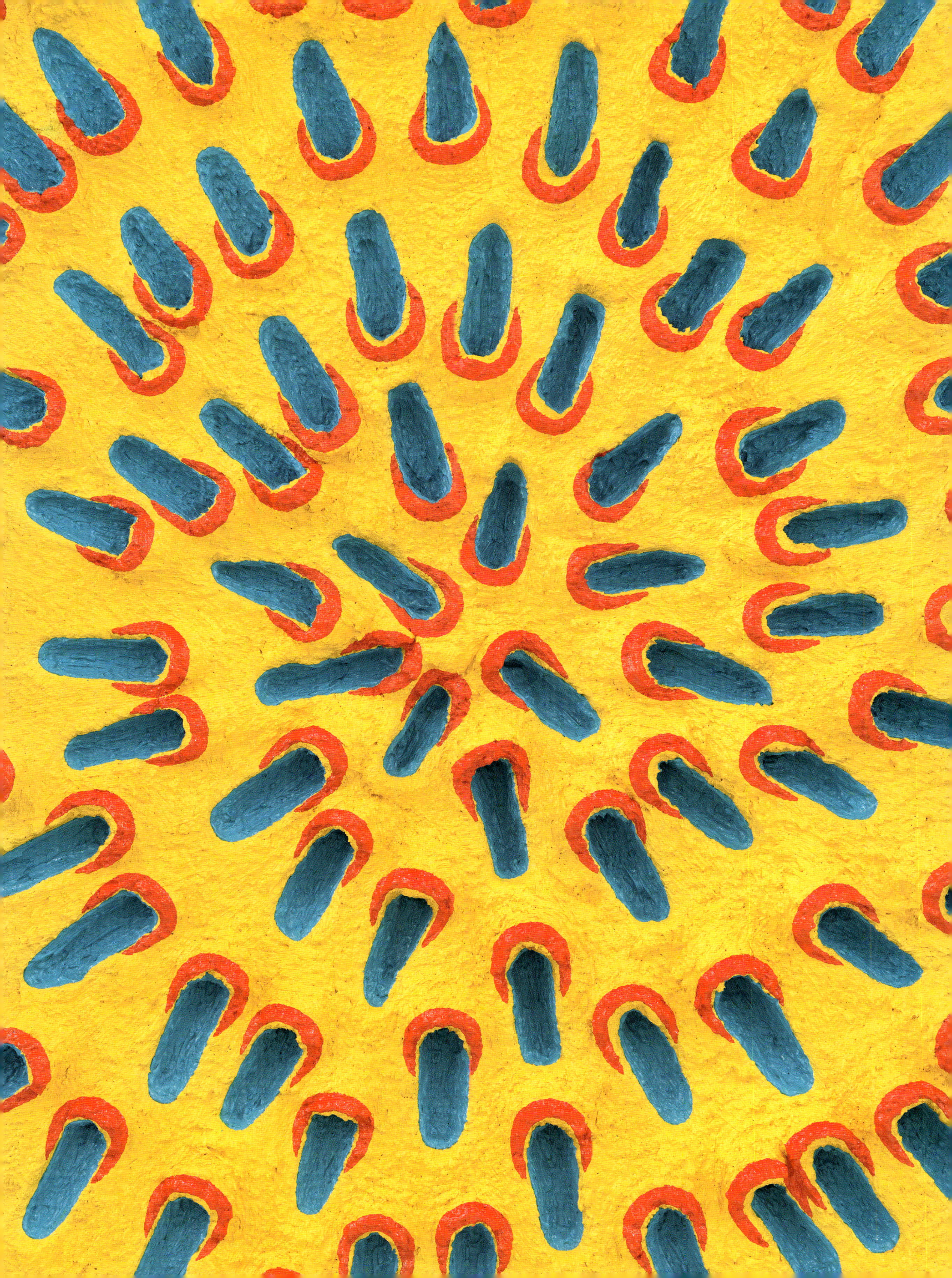

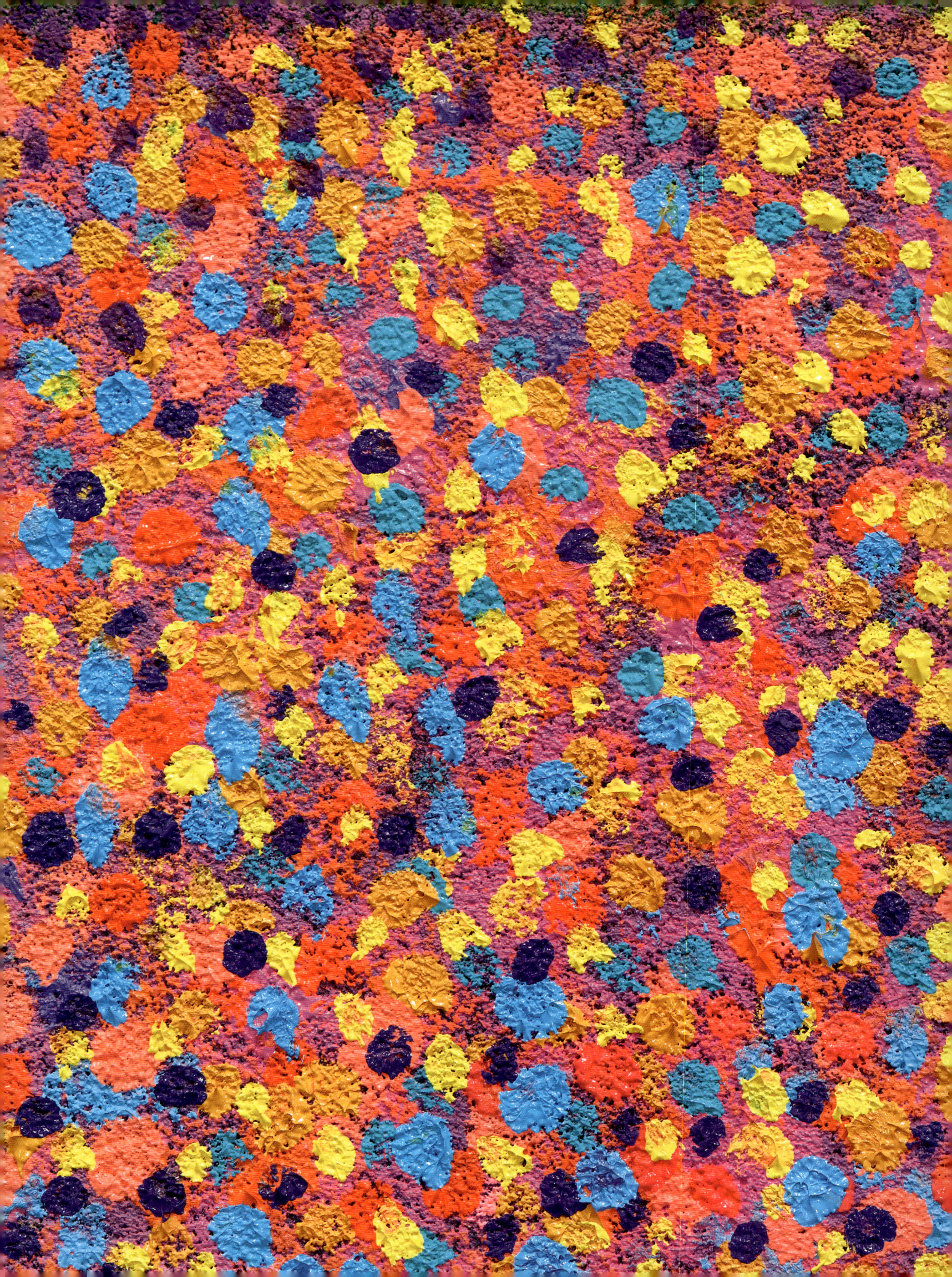

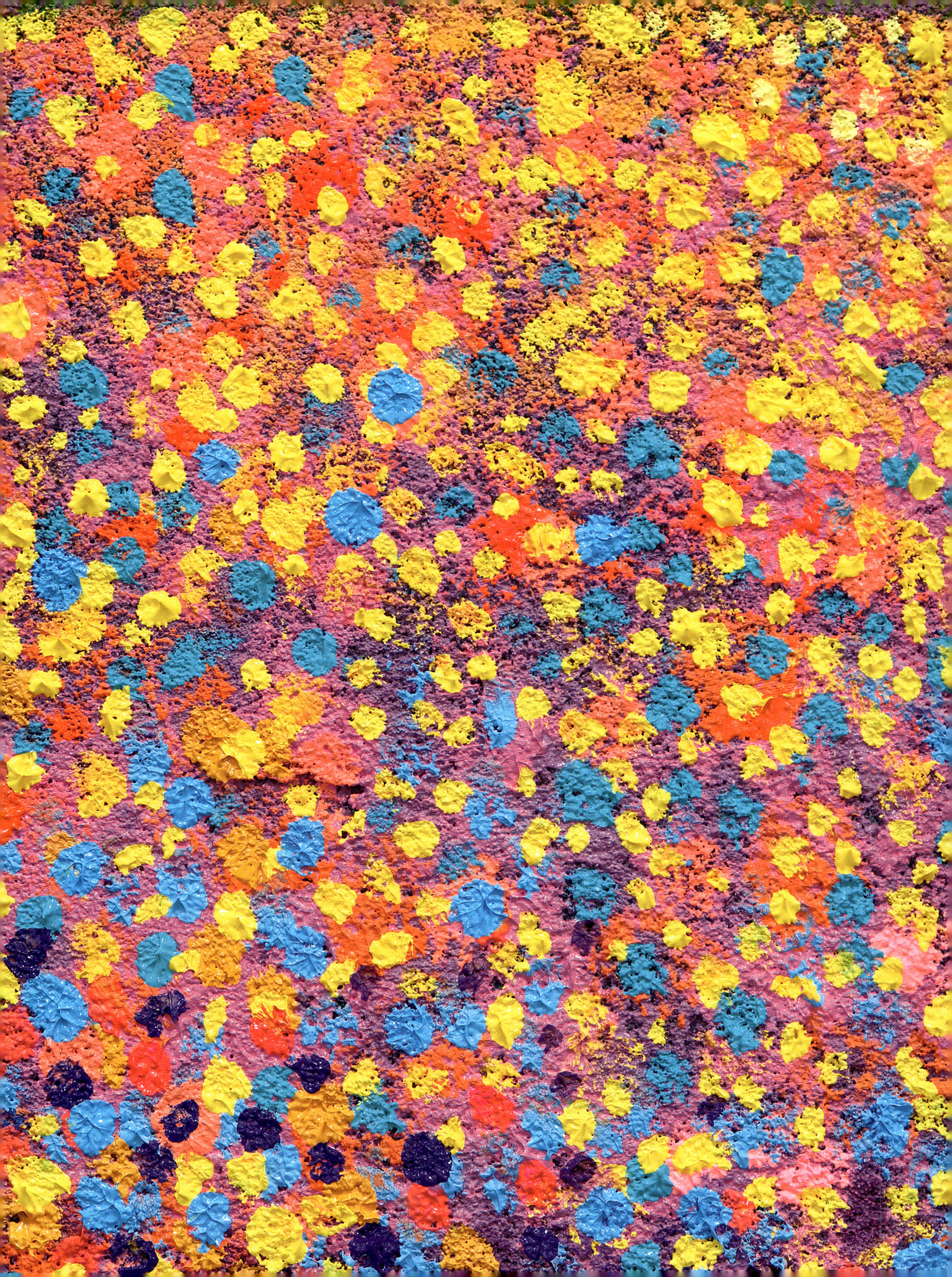

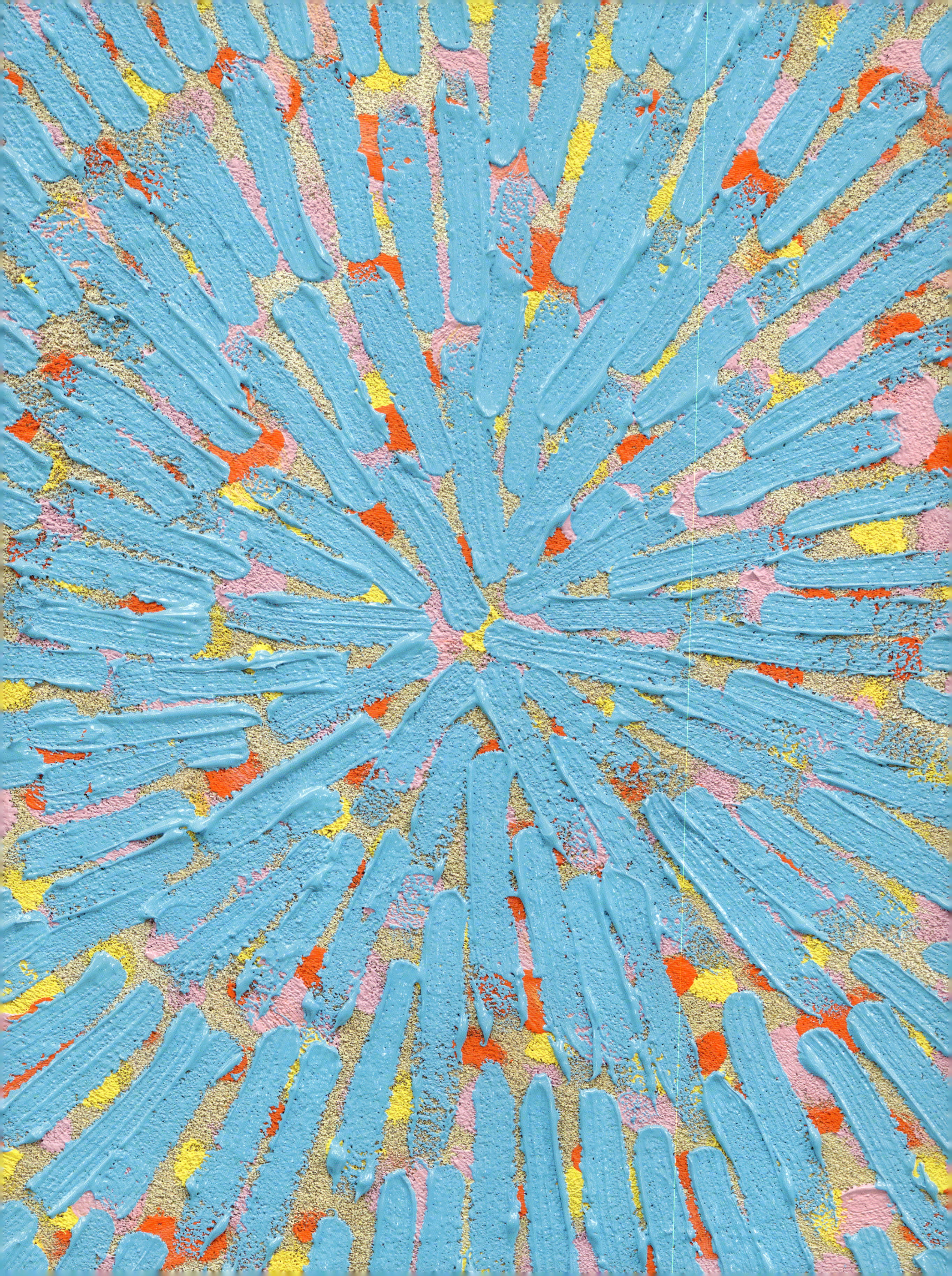

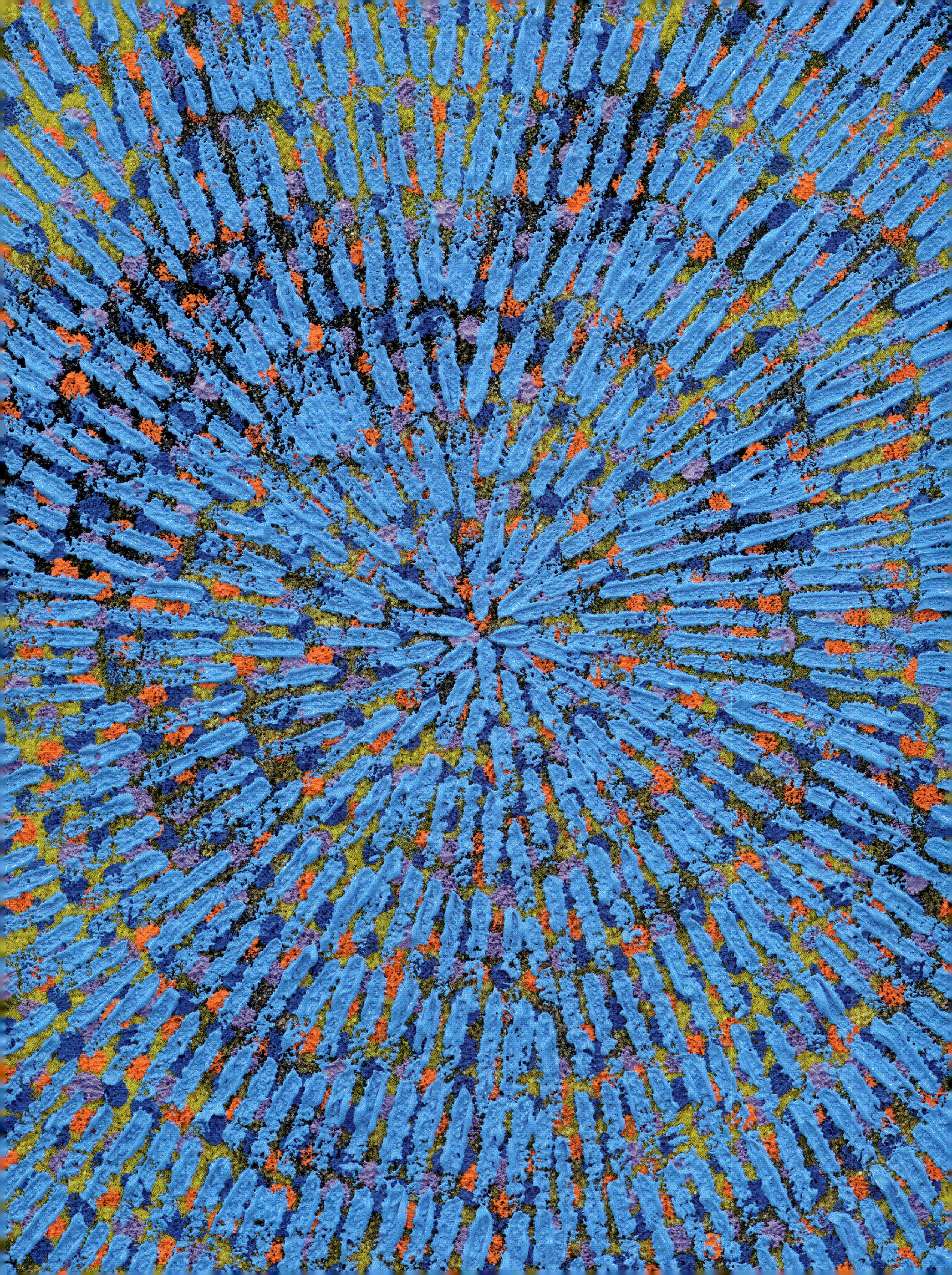

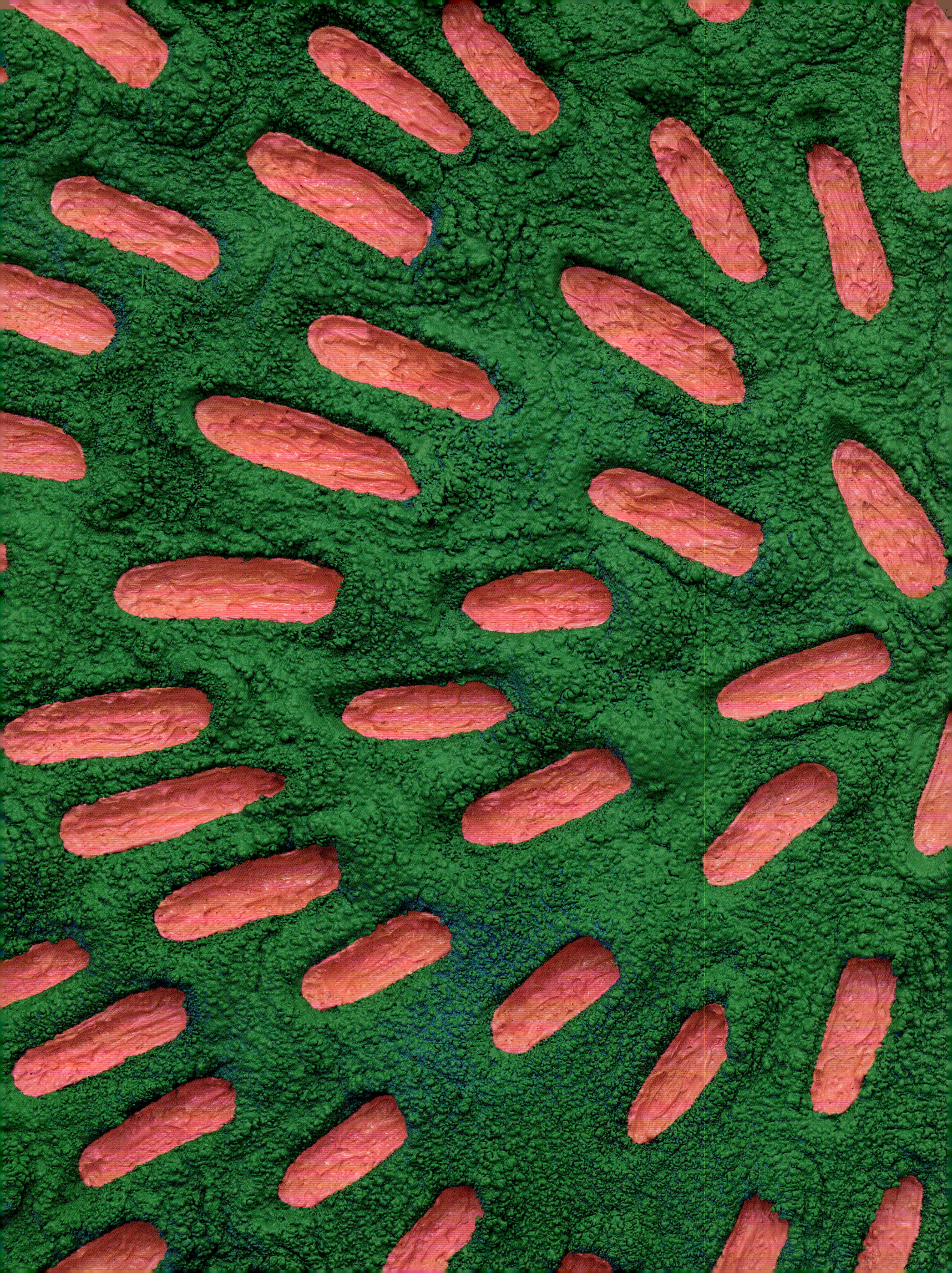

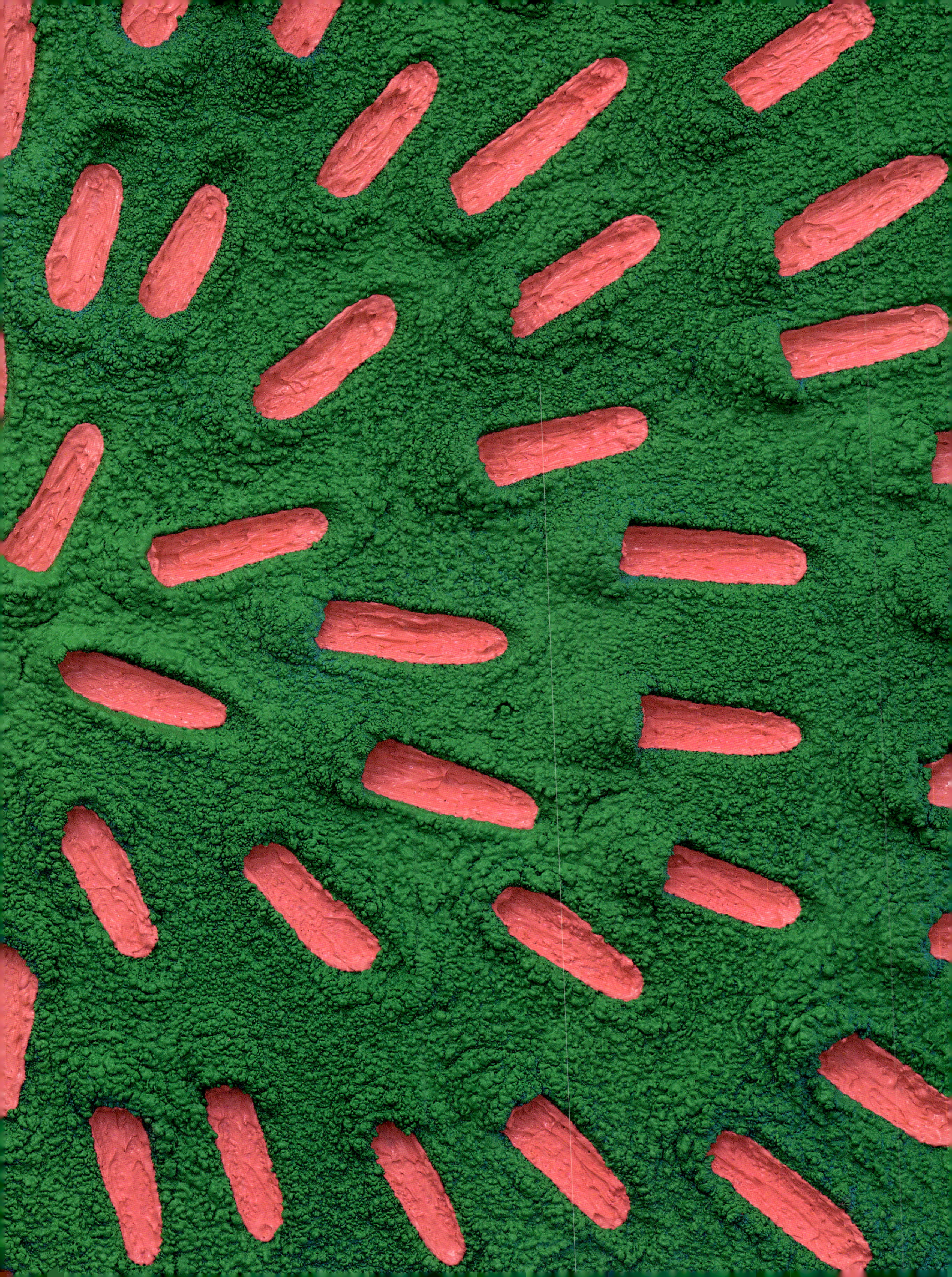

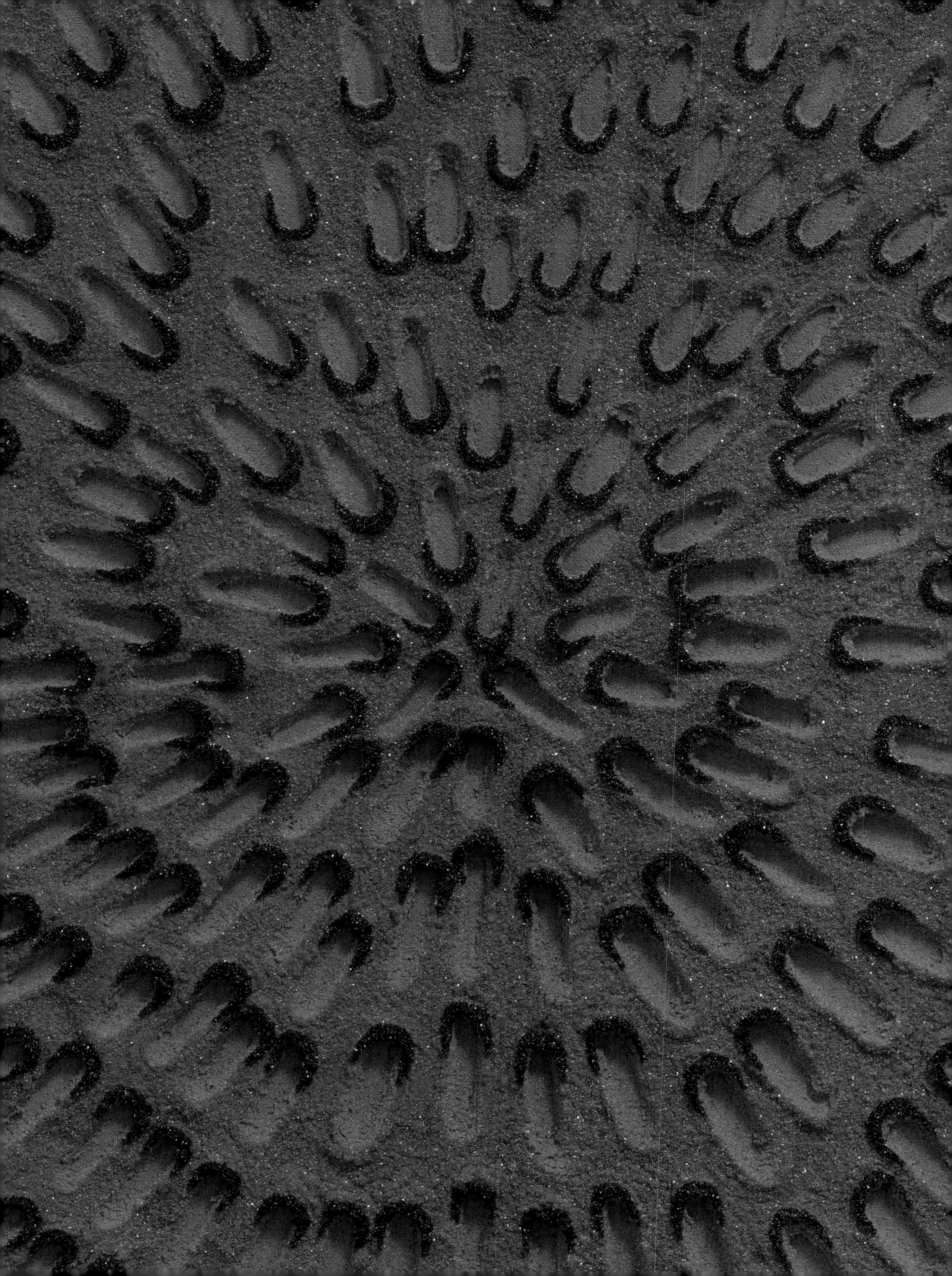

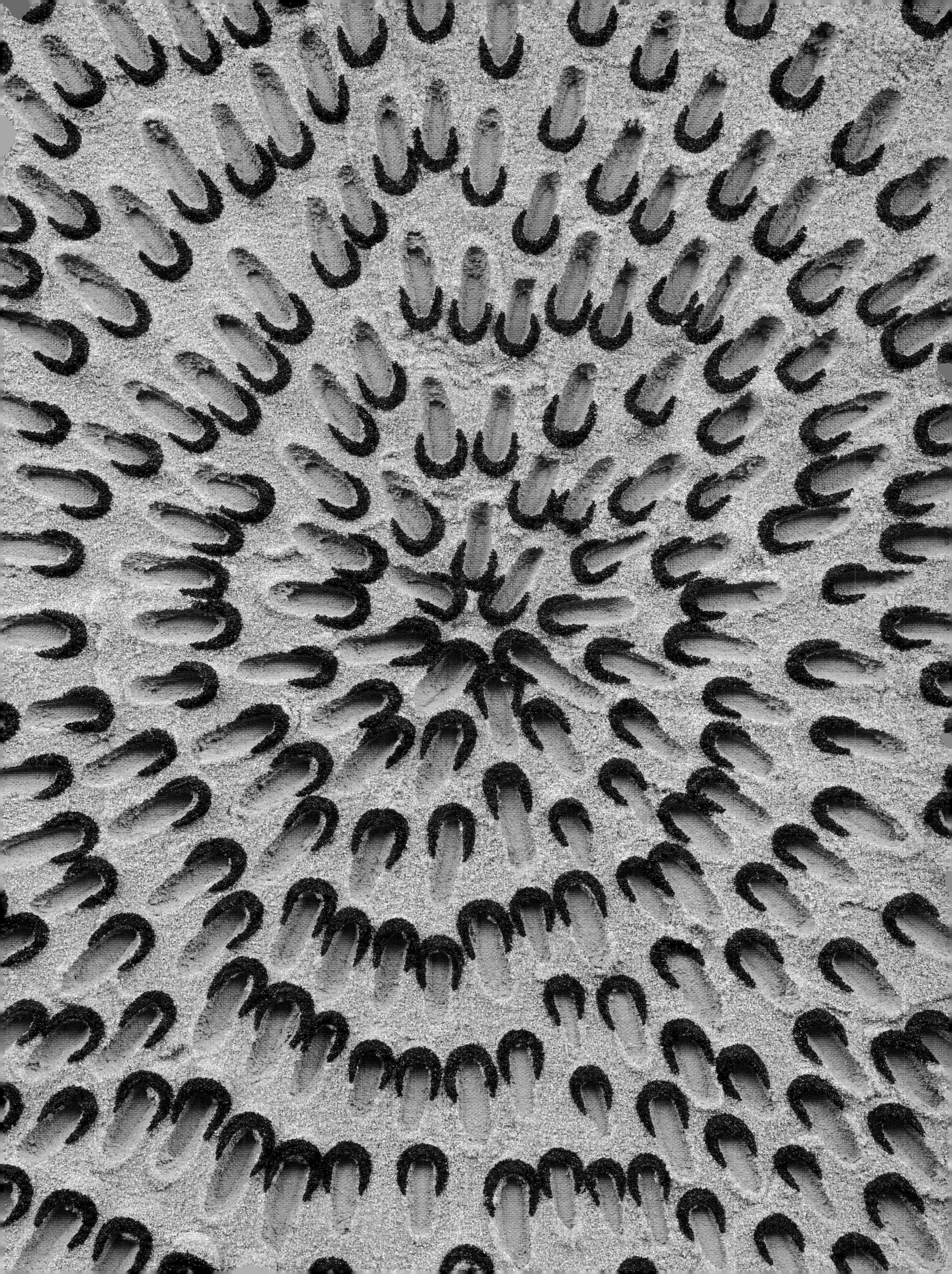

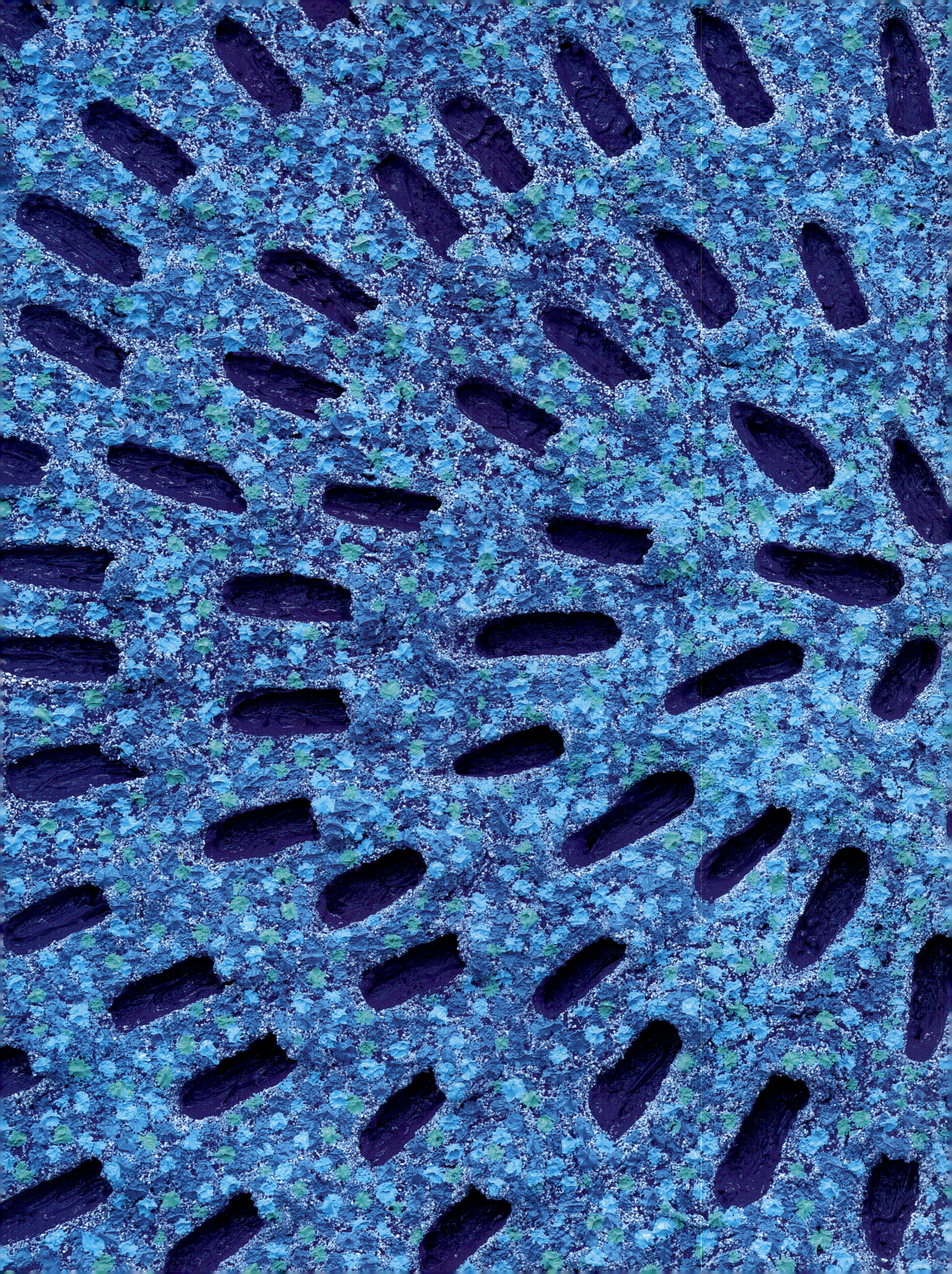

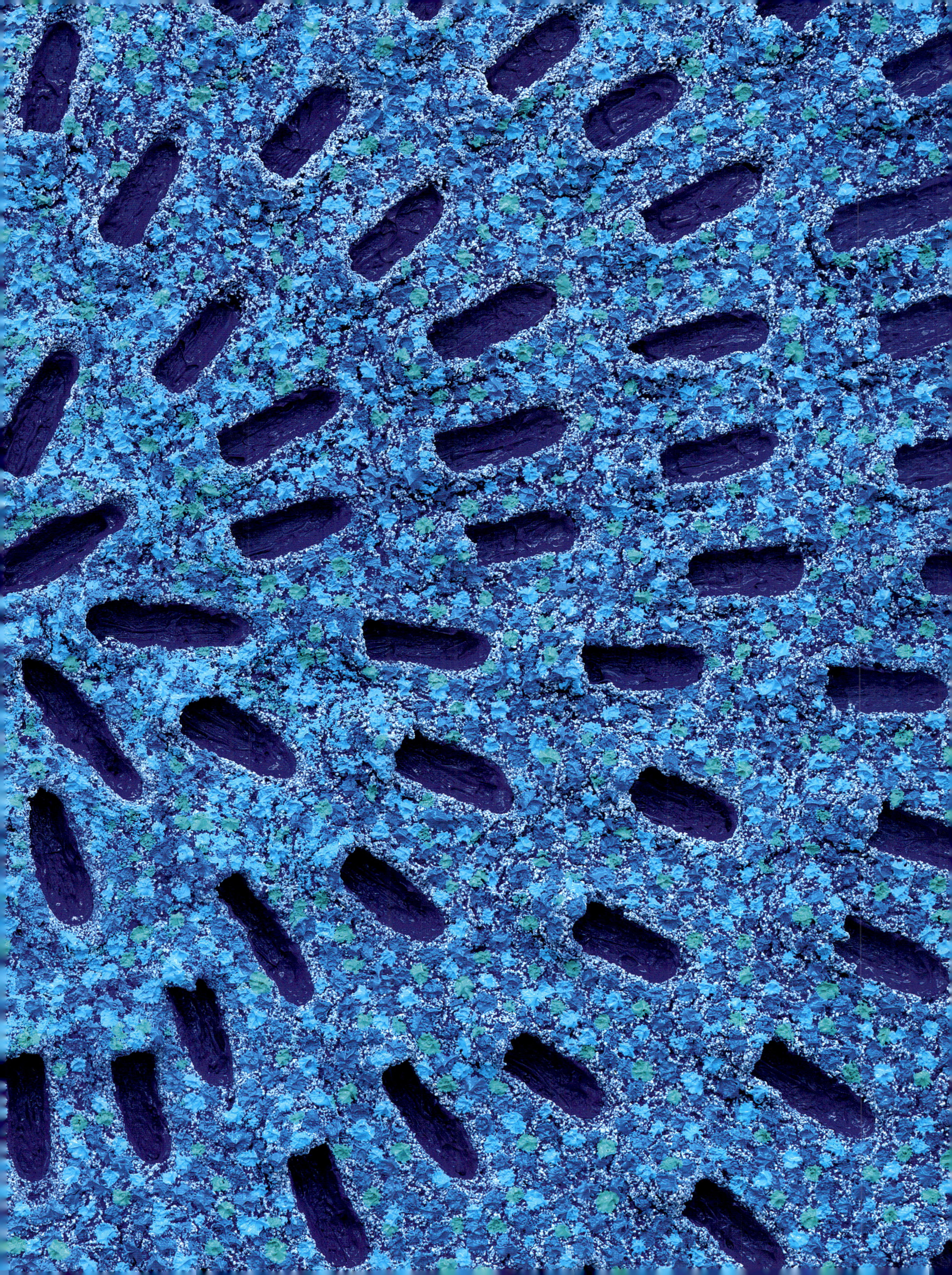

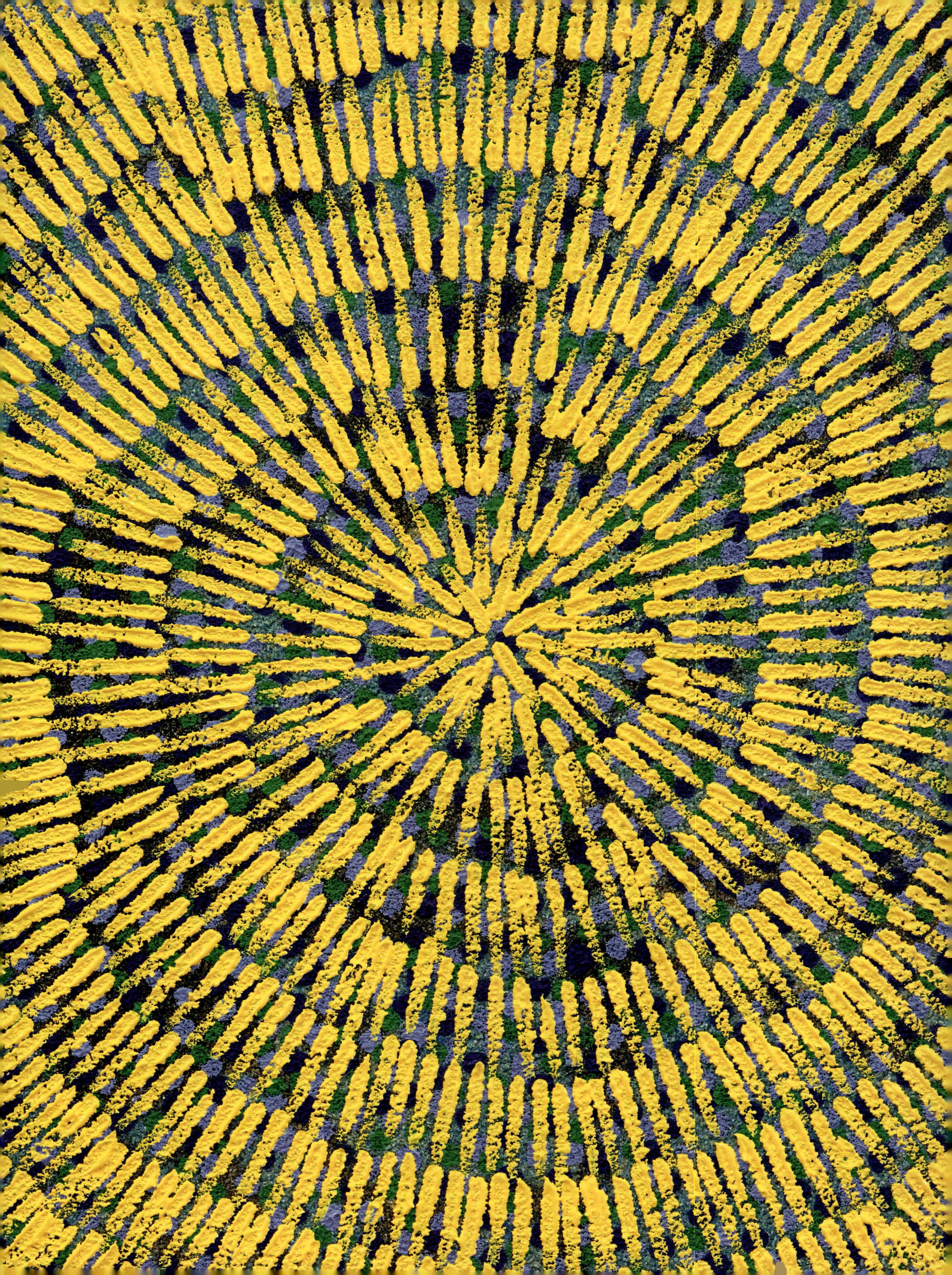

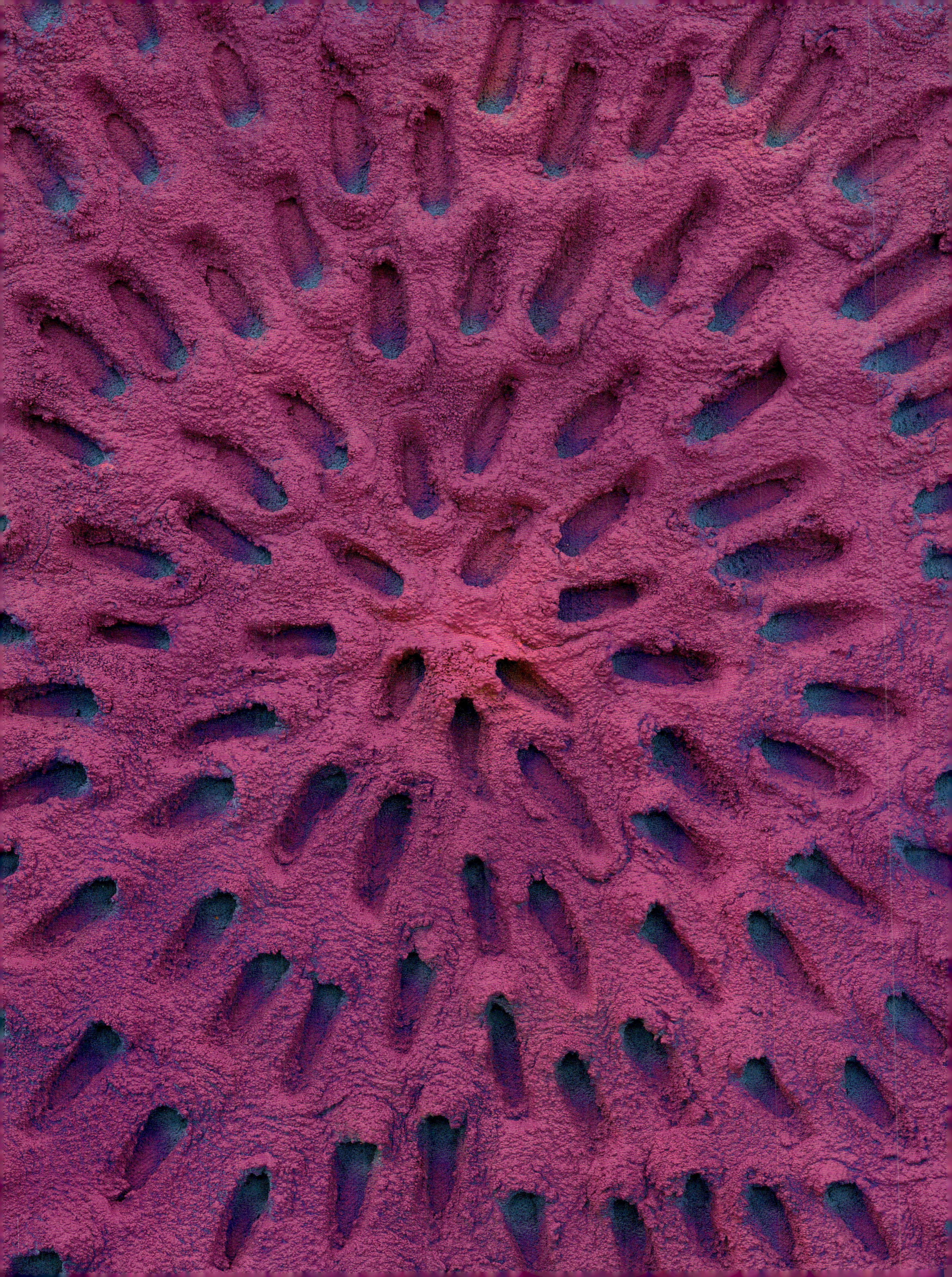

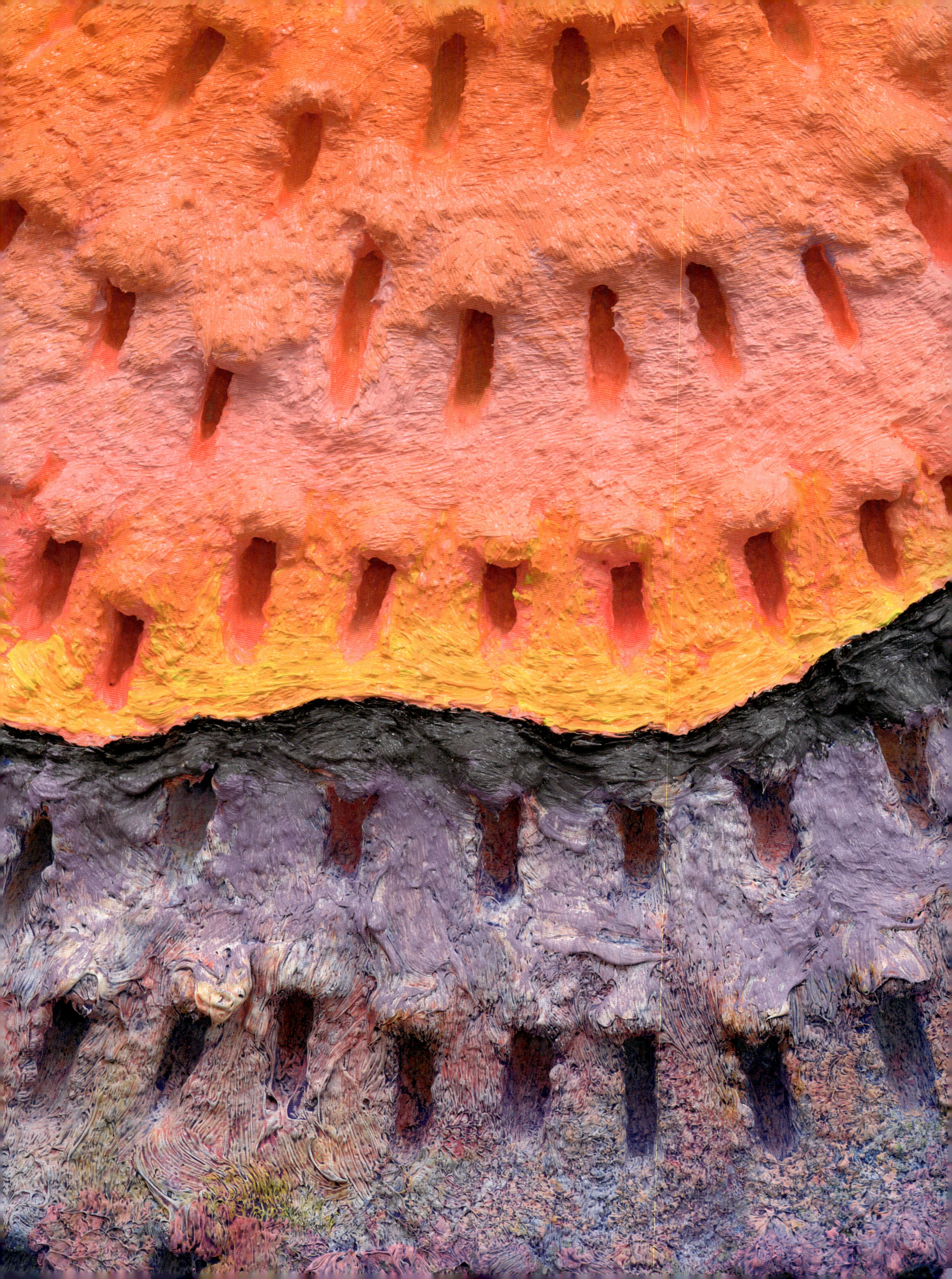

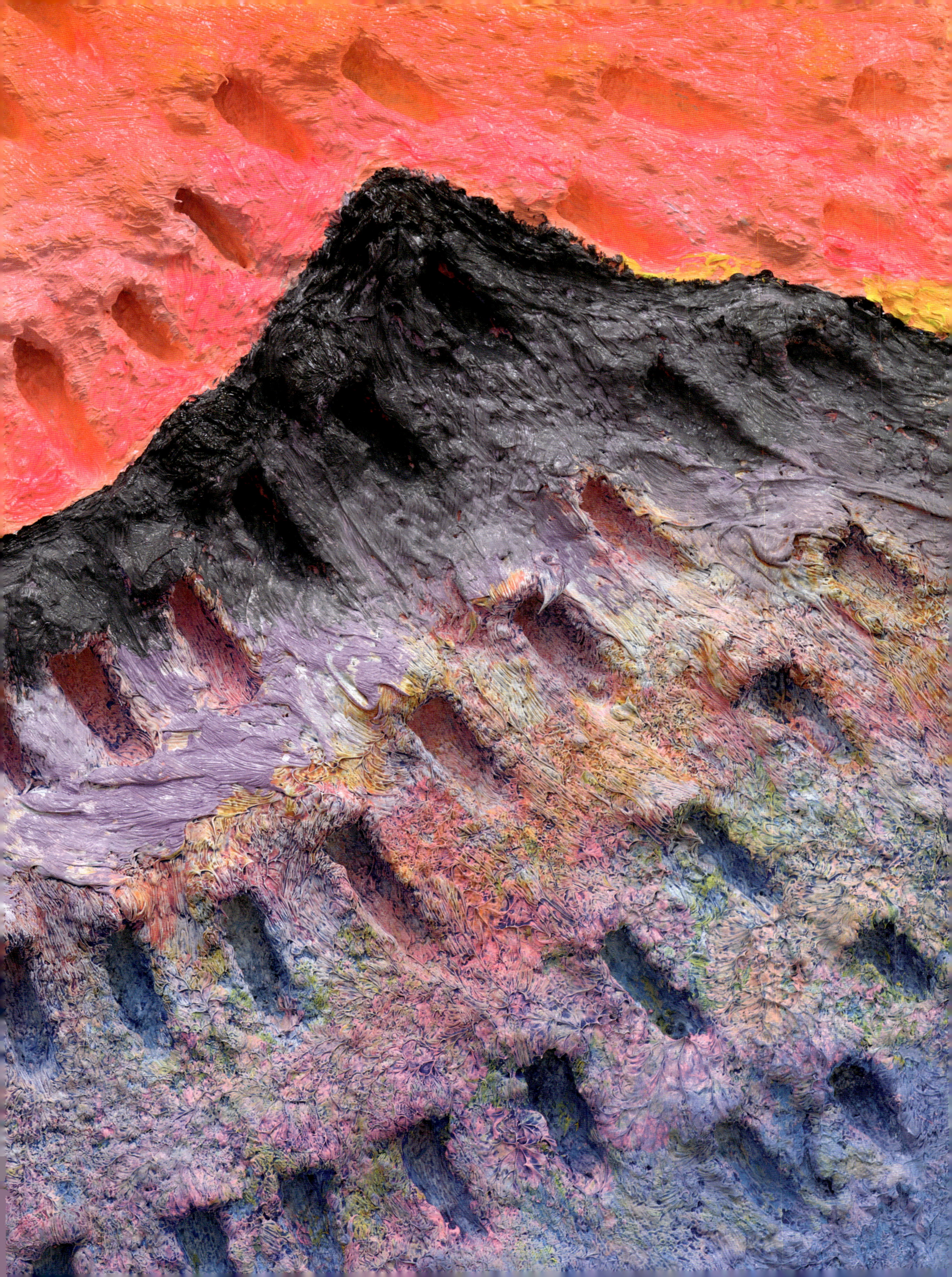

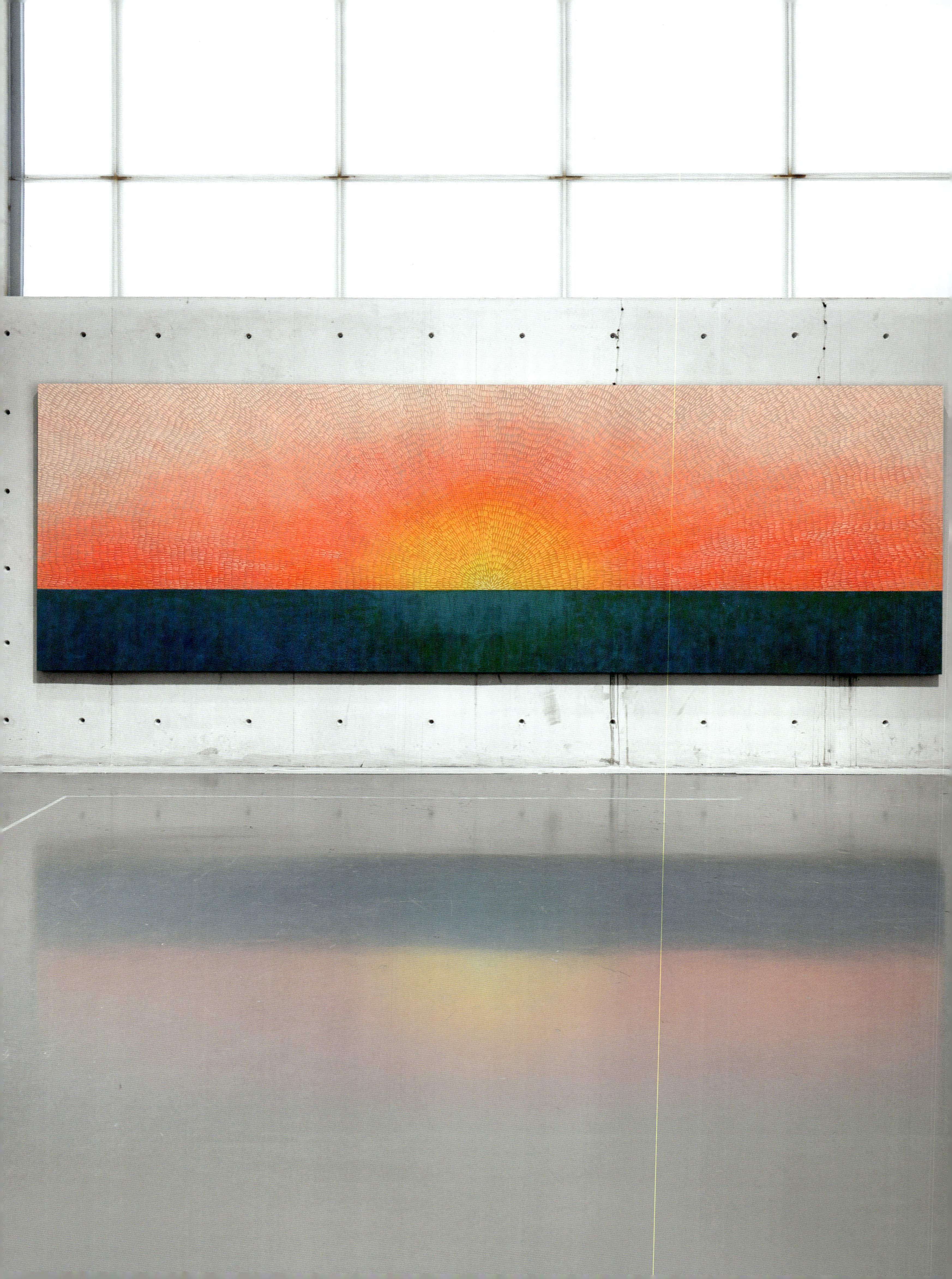

Biography

Jennifer Guidi was born in 1972 in Redondo Beach, California. She received a BFA from Boston University and an MFA from the School of the Art Institute of Chicago.

Guidi's work is included in many important public and private collections worldwide, including the Dallas Museum of Art; de la Cruz Collection, Miami; Hammer Museum, Los Angeles; Los Angeles County Museum of Art; Louis Vuitton Foundation, Paris; Marciano Art Foundation, Los Angeles; Museum of Contemporary Art, Los Angeles; Rubell Family Collection, Miami; Sammlung Goetz, Munich; San Francisco Museum of Modern Art; and Solomon R. Guggenheim Museum, New York.

Recent solo exhibitions include *Rituals*, Gagosian, New York (2024); *And so it is.*, Orange County Museum of Art, Costa Mesa, CA (2023); *Mountain Range*, Château La Coste, Provence (2023); *In the Heart of the Sun*, David Kordansky Gallery, Los Angeles (2022); *Full Moon*, Long Museum West Bund, Shanghai (2022); *Points of Harmony*, MASSIMODECARLO, Pièce Unique, Paris (2021); *Gemini*, Gagosian, New York (2020); *Eclipse*, MASSIMODECARLO, Belgioioso, Milan (2019); *Heliocentric* at Gagosian, Hong Kong (2018); *More Life*, David Kordansky Gallery, Los Angeles (2017); and *Visible Light/Luce Visibile*, Museo d'Arte Contemporanea Villa Croce, Genoa (2017).

Selected group exhibitions include *20*, David Kordansky Gallery, Los Angeles (2023); *Together, at the Same Time*, de la Cruz Collection, Miami (2022); *Artists Inspired by Music: Interscope Reimagined*, Los Angeles County Museum of Art, Los Angeles (2022); *Beatitudes of Malibu*, David Kordansky Gallery, Los Angeles (2021); *An Ideal Landscape*, Gagosian, New York (2021); *L.A.*, Maki Collection, Tokyo (2020); *Inner Realm*, MASSIMODECARLO, V Space (2020); *From Day to Day*, de la Cruz Collection, Miami (2019); *One Day at a Time: Manny Farber and Termite Art*, Museum of Contemporary Art, Los Angeles (2018); *Generations: Female Artists in Dialogue*, Part 1, Sammlung Goetz, Haus der Kunst, Munich (2018); *Unpacking: The Marciano Collection*, Marciano Art Foundation, Los Angeles (2017); *No Man's Land: Women Artists from the Rubell Family Collection*, Rubell Family Collection, Miami (2015, traveled to the National Museum of Women in the Arts, Washington, DC, through 2016); and *The Afghan Carpet Project*, Hammer Museum, Los Angeles (2015).

Guidi lives and works in Los Angeles.